At the close of the events at the March on Washington f
Freedom, as 250,000 Americans at the Lincoln Memorial cheered and wiped tears from their cheeks, and as millions at home shared their proud reactions to seeing it on TV, Bayard Rustin's voice was the last one heard from the stage. Pledge cards like the one shown here were passed out to people at the March. Shown here is Maxwell Whittington-Cooper as John Lewis in *Rustin*, reading one of the cards. Rustin led the audience through a recitation of a pledge to make a commitment to what we then called "the struggle." The pledge not only affirms a commitment to peaceful protest, and to vote, but to involve others to seek justice "through the courts and the legislative process." He not only told them the baton was being passed but gave it to us in writing. His specifics comprise a list of areas for our vigilance and commitment six decades later, because they are the voices and tools of creating justice. Please take a look, as John Lewis did.

PLEDGE Standing before the Lincoln Memorial on the 28th of August, in the Centennial Year of Emancipation, I affirm my complete personal commitment to the struggle for Jobs and Freedom for all Americans.

To fulfill that commitment, I pledge that I will not relax until victory is won.

I pledge that I will join and

RUSTIN

THULANI DAVIS

RUSTIN

A FILM BY
GEORGE C. WOLFE

ASSOULINE

TABLE OF CONTENTS

SEAL OF THE PRESIDENT OF THE UNITED STATES

PRESIDENT BARACK OBAMA, 2013 PRESIDENTIAL MEDAL OF FREEDOM CEREMONY

"Bayard Rustin was a giant in the American Civil Rights Movement. Openly gay at a time when many had to hide who they loved, his unwavering belief that we are all equal members of a 'single human family' took him from his first Freedom Ride to the lesbian, gay, bisexual and transgender rights movement. Thanks to his unparalleled skills as an organizer, progress that once seemed impossible appears, in retrospect, to have been inevitable. Fifty years after the March on Washington he organized, America honors Bayard Rustin as one of its greatest architects for social change and a fearless advocate for its most vulnerable citizens."

President Barack Obama speaks at a dinner in honor of the Medal of Freedom awardees at the Smithsonian National Museum of American History in Washington, D.C., 2013.

INTRODUCTION:
THE ULTIMATE AMERICAN

BY GEORGE C. WOLFE

Having lived inside the mind, the accomplishments, and the astonishing legacy that is Bayard Rustin, casually for the past thirty years as an admirer, and intensely so for the past four, crafting a film about him, there is one event, incidental yet revelatory which fills me with unabashed joy.

No, not the fact that he was the mastermind of the March on Washington, and together with the assistance of a group of kids in their late-teens, early-twenties, organized the largest peaceful protest the world had ever known. And not the fact that he traveled to India to study the practices and teachings of non-violence as espoused by Mahatma Gandhi, which he in-turn shared with innumerable colleagues, including his close friend and mentee, Martin Luther King Jr. And not the fact that Bayard Rustin was one of the most, if not *the* most, "out" versions of an out homosexual to be found walking the streets of New York City from the 1940s on, or appeared on Broadway in the chorus of *John Henry,* a musical of epic proportions starring Paul Robeson, which opened on January 10th, 1940, and closed five performances later.

No, the one event in Bayard's life that to this day causes me to quizzically, giddily shout to myself, "You've got to be kidding!" is that, in between fighting to save the soul of his country, he managed to find time to record an album entitled *Elizabethan Songs & Negro Spirituals,* which, point of fact, featured <u>the</u> Bayard Rustin singing, in that crystalline tenor of his, both Elizabethan songs and Negro spirituals.

The reason this piece of vinyl thrills me to no end is because it brilliantly captures the expansive view he had of himself and his place in the world, or should I say worlds, which existed in joyful defiance of other people's limited view of who he was, where he belonged and what he should desire. And it is for this reason, among a myriad of others, that Black-queer-Quaker Bayard Taylor Rustin is, to my mind, the ultimate American.

An accomplished tenor vocalist, Bayard Rustin released an LP in 1952 titled *Elizabethan Songs & Negro Spirituals.*

with harpsichord accompaniment by

MARGARET DAVISON

Elizabethan SONGS

with harpsichord accompaniment

I Attempt from Love's Sickness to Fly
Have You Seen But a Whyte Lillie Grow?
Cara e Dolce
Flow My Tears
The Lass with the Delicate air

with lute accompaniment

I Saw Her As I Came and Went
Ah, the Sighs that Come from My Heart
Gather Ye Rosebuds While Ye May

Negro SPIRITUALS

Swing Low, Sweet Chariot
Nobody Knows the Trouble I've Seen
Ezekiel Saw a Wheel
There Is a Balm in Gilead

A FELLOWSHIP Long-Playing Record

My definition of being an American does not begin with amber waves of grain, nor ends with red, white and blue bunting on the Fourth, but one which has at its core a sense of service, expansive curiosity, and caring for those in need.

Bayard was born in 1912, in West Chester, Pennsylvania. He was not only his high school's valedictorian, but the West Chester Warrior's star athlete; track, football, tennis, basketball, he did it all, and took to heart the school's moniker, becoming a warrior on and off the field. Despite its legacy of being a stop on the Underground Railroad, by the time Bayard was in his mid-teens, Jim Crow–isms had firmly infiltrated Chester County, which Bayard rabidly took on, organizing sit-ins at movie theaters, the YMCA, restaurants, informing one of his coaches that unless he and the other Black members of the team stayed in the same accommodations as their white counterparts during away games, they would not play.

And when he was sent to prison during World War II, for being a conscientious objector, on "moral, religious, and political grounds," the warden, after failing repeatedly to stop Bayard's hunger strikes, endless acts of insubordination, and demands that segregation within the United States penal system be abolished, realized the only solution was to have Bayard transferred to another penitentiary.

It is this very sense of defiance, determination and heart that one feels when you hear him sing on *Elizabethan Songs & Negro Spirituals;* the compassion and caring in his rendition of "There Is a Balm in Gilead," the isolation yet strength on "I Attempt from Love's Sickness to Fly."

Back when he was playing offensive lineman for the West Chester Warriors, the story goes, he would aggressively knock an opposing player to the ground, and then graciously help him to his feet. This dichotomy was equally embedded in everything he undertook, including the planning of The March.

In addition to his desire to cast an unswerving light on the legacy of segregation, which despite the passage of *Brown vs. Board of Education,* continued to flourish in the South, Bayard also wanted to bring people together; bring the divergent Civil Rights Organizations that were starting to fracture together; bring the country as a whole together.

Fearless, defiant, celebratory, demanding, unrelenting, collaborative, exceedingly curious, and smarter than smart, because of all of the above, he is for me the ultimate American, what every American should strive to be. I am grateful for and forever in awe of all that he accomplished, and deeply proud, as is everyone who worked on the making of *RUSTIN,* to share his remarkable story with the world, and with you.

Bayard Rustin and Cleveland Robinson shortly before the March on Washington, 1963.

SNCC

MARCH ON WASHINGTON
JOBS & FREEDOM

EPUT
U.S.
RSHA

JOBS

THE ONE WHO HOPES WE WILL KEEP SHOWING UP

BAYARD RUSTIN

The film *Rustin,* directed by George C. Wolfe and produced by Bruce Cohen, Tonia Davis, and George C. Wolfe, in association with President Barack Obama and Michelle Obama's Higher Ground Productions, takes us into the life of Bayard Rustin, the extraordinary architect of nonviolent change in this country. We view the breadth of his life's work through the prism of a taut drama taking place inside the command center of an outlandishly optimistic, unrealistically timed, and tactically brilliant operation that became the massive and joyous moment we know as the March on Washington for Jobs and Freedom in 1963. Many will be encountering for the first time the Black, gay philosopher-strategist Rustin, who was asked to stand in the shadows of his most dramatic accomplishment in making change in the United States. It is the story of that man that the team behind the film was eager to tell.

When Bayard Rustin was born in 1912, he was named after a poet and diplomat from his hometown. The Quaker practices he was taught by his mother, who was a Quaker, and the larger community in West Chester, Pennsylvania, required listening and leaving moments of silence before responding to what others said. Such training early in life might cause a person to find it amusing to listen to someone who is just posturing. Or unbearably tiresome. He was also raised in the African Methodist Episcopal Church of his father and learned to honor the passion of the spirit and the patience needed for generational change and processing the handed-down traumas of slavery. And in a circumstance created by discrimination in the North for Black travelers, as a young person he sometimes discovered William Edward Burghardt Du Bois, James Weldon Johnson, or Mary McLeod Bethune, Black visionaries, at the breakfast table as honored guests in his grandparents' home, where he was raised.[1] The home in which he grew up, like those of many Blacks his age, was a repository of firsthand knowledge of the slavery system. Bayard Rustin's impatient drive to make change, which came early, was leavened by an upbringing that guided him to respect his own ideas and still be patient with others trying to find change in themselves. By the time of his death in 1987, Rustin had helped build movements of many types, around issues of justice—racial, economic, voting rights, labor rights—and peace.

Bayard Rustin in New York City a few weeks before the March on Washington, 1963.

Bayard Rustin at his Park Avenue South office in New York City, 1969.

He was never able to adjust to the prevalence and normalcy of cruelty in this country. Nonviolent protest was the sanest response he could see to the prevalence of American violence. He concluded we must make others see the violence that is treated as normal. For Rustin, that violence against decency and self-respect was segregation, the violence against one's chances in life stemming from poverty, lack of decent housing, poor access to medical care, war, and nuclear weapons. And those forms of violence are still made tolerable by the publicly accepted violence against Black and Brown bodies by police or neighbors, and fed by the rumors across the culture that people of color are coming for their jobs, their partners, their children, and their place in society, or their lives. For Rustin, it was vital that all citizens be able to use their right to vote if they were to protect all their other rights.

Bayard Rustin, like most people, probably didn't learn most of this in his formal education. He first went to the country's oldest historically Black college or university (HBCU), Wilberforce, where he had objections to the required Reserve Officers' Training Corps (ROTC) training—an issue that students at other HBCUs would still be fighting as late as 1968. Ahead of his time, maybe. He then went to Quaker-founded Cheyney State University, where the antiwar movement of the day took hold, and he also began to renew his Quaker practice with "daily quiet periods for guidance."[2] According to the editors of the book *Time on Two Crosses: The Collected Writings of Bayard Rustin,* Rustin was expelled from Cheyney when administrators "learned of his sexual orientation."[3] But with only a few more credits to earn, he left for New York City. He did not start at City College right away, as his family had hoped, but when he did, he also got involved in protests over the group of young men known as the Scottsboro Boys, wrongly accused of rape in Alabama. He joined the Young Communist League but shortly decided it was not for him.[4] And as an accomplished singer, he gigged at Cafe Society in its heyday, likely with Josh White, which would have been an education in the sublime, since that's where Billie Holiday first sang "Strange Fruit," while she was playing there for nine months. Any young adult who could hear Lady Day, Big Joe Turner, and Sarah Vaughan on the regular would be apt to land somewhere between poet and diplomat.[5]

By 1941, Rustin had met two people working with labor groups who would have a profound influence on him: A. Philip Randolph, president of the Brotherhood of Sleeping Car Porters, and A. J. Muste, a pacifist who ran the Fellowship of Reconciliation (FOR). Rustin admired Randolph for his ability to organize Black workers and took to Muste's spiritually based pacifism and advocacy of nonviolence. The three men organized the 1941 March on Washington, to protest against segregation in the armed forces and employment

Bayard Rustin with a map detailing the path of the March on Washington during a news conference at the New York City headquarters just a few days before the March in 1963.

“Sometimes a person like Rustin might get pegged as ahead of his time when he is right on time.”

THULANI DAVIS

Wednesday
August 28, 1963

MARCH ON WASHINGTON FOR JOBS AND FREEDOM
170 West 130 Street
New York 27, New York
FIlmore 8-1900

MEMO

Founding Chairmen
James Farmer
Martin Luther King
John Lewis
A. Philip Randolph
Roy Wilkins
Whitney Young

Administrative Committee
Cleveland Robinson
Chairman
Courtland Cox
Ann Arnold Hedgeman
Rev. Thomas Kilgore, Jr.
Rev. George Lawrence
James McCain
Dr. John Morsell
Guichard Parris

Director
A. Philip Randolph

Deputy Director
Bayard Rustin

Coordinators
Norman Hill
L. Joseph Overton

Southern Administrators
Dr. Aaron Henry
Worth Long
Att. Floyd McKissick
Rev. Wyatt Walker

To: Bayard
From: Courtland
Re: Southern Freedom Trains

I have communicated with the various railroads asking for a written reply which would give the reasons for the lack of the transportation facilities for the March. I also included in the letter a statement concerning our intentions to send copies of their letters to the I. C. C.

When they send their replies I suggest that a statement be released to the press and/or a telegram to Robert Kennedy stating the following:

1) Participants will be travelling through the South for long distances and much of the travelling will be done at night through areas that have been known to be dangerous for travel when buses or cars transporting Negroes or an integrated group have risked travelling through these areas.

2) If we are not able to secure the transportation facilities of the railroads we have no choice but to use buses and cars for transportation to Washington.

3) The possibility of injury to our participants is therefore greatly increased and if this possibility becomes a reality, as we know it will, the United States government would be placed in a very embarassing and dangerous position.

4) Therefore, we are asking that you inform the railroads as to the possible dangers involved in not making trains available to the March Committee.

P.S. You might call Martin King and ask him if ~~(would)~~ he has secured the train from Coastline railroad. If he has not impress upon him the importance of reserving that train.

Letter to Bayard Rustin from Courtland Cox about transportation to the March.
Opposite: Bayard Rustin meets with March marshals ahead of the March on Washington in 1963.

discrimination, and then canceled it after getting President Franklin D. Roosevelt to go as far as banning discrimination in defense industries and in federal agencies. During World War II, Rustin traveled through twenty states for FOR, visited camps where conscientious objectors were sent, and in California visited the Manzanar internment camp, helping Japanese-American families who had been imprisoned there. While working for Muste's group, Rustin also met James Farmer and the two other founders of the Congress of Racial Equality (CORE) helping them to organize the nonviolent resistance group. In 1942, on a bus trip from Louisville to Nashville, Rustin refused to sit in the back of the bus and was arrested as seen in the film. He took several beatings for it, starting on the bus in front of all the passengers. According to one biographer, several passengers tried to get the police to stop the beating and one went to the police station to support his view of resisting an unjust law.

Sometimes a person like Rustin might get pegged as ahead of his time when he is right on time. One of the problems is that too many Americans have been taught too little of the past to judge what time it is. "How long?" asked Rev. Martin Luther King Jr. in 1965, speaking to activists gathered at the end of the last march from Selma to Montgomery. "How long?" Each time he asked, the crowd said, "Too long." Bayard Rustin was sitting on that makeshift stage as King opened the call-and-response.[6] Rustin, a man deeply moved by Gandhi's nonviolence, had found a ready listener in Dr. King, a contemplative young man, and yet throughout his life he had to prove its power to most others he met. But by the time they marched from Selma to Montgomery for voting rights, Rustin had persuaded folks across the nation that they could show that power. Though Black newspapers had routinely covered and cheered on Gandhi's movement when Rustin was in college, perhaps that memory was gone by the early 1950s. People may have thought it of no relevance that India achieved independence with nonviolent action. Was Rustin ahead of his time? No, right on time. He gave young protesters a simple instruction—"bring cameras"—to make sure that people saw what happened to bodies making change. He didn't necessarily bother to explain that the cameras in India let the world see injustice. Southern protests were daunting. People in the local police force might prepare for Blacks to act violently, as he discovered in Washington, D.C., even though the cameras in the South had shown them the real worry—nonviolence met by clubs, fire hoses, or an unpoliced mob threatening to lynch a teenage girl for trying to enter a local high school.

A man might have come into adulthood comfortable with loving men, and yet find people want him shunned because they don't want to see it. People might say he is too far ahead of his time because that is what they think they know. Director George C. Wolfe puts it this way: "For lack of better words, all conversations about liberation, all conversations about owning one's power, are one and the same. The specifics are very different, but it became really interesting to focus in on the fact that Bayard was sophisticated and yet still imprisoned by people's reaction to it."

Of course, Bayard Rustin knew nonviolent protesters needed cameras to be there because he took more than one of those beatings in a dark place with no witnesses. And because he was where he was and took the beating and jail time he got, we have learned that only with video can we get convictions for people killed while lying in the street, not resisting, or lying in bed at home. A student of Gandhi showed us that gathering in peace could get the government to commit to the Civil Rights Act of 1964 and the Voting Rights Act of 1965. In the film *Rustin*, we see how Rustin managed all that and cooked Indian food for Ella Baker and drank in a bar where men looked in each other's eyes with Ruth Brown singing on the jukebox. As one who urged King not to withdraw from marching from Selma to Montgomery, he taught us that the deaths of Jimmie Lee Jackson and Reverend James Reeb and Viola Liuzzo during those marches should never be banned from history classes in American schools, as they gave their lives because change was on time. Bayard Rustin helped people put change in their sights. For us southerners, some of that change was sudden and useful—a day in 1965 when one could, for the first time, walk into a public library and take out a book. Other change needed then is still easily seen now. Six years after the March, Rustin saw the Stonewall Uprising take place in New York in 1969. In recent years we've seen a rise of attacks on such gathering places. Rustin the organizer is still on time in an era when driving while Black or ringing the wrong doorbell can result in death. Still, Bayard Rustin was among us in towns small and large, some of them towns with hardly a single Black resident, as marchers went peacefully into the streets across the country during a deadly pandemic to protest the murder of George Floyd in Minneapolis. Whole families, sheltered at home due to COVID, happened to witness Floyd's death. In days like these, when the groups that have always been targeted by hate are being shot at during public gatherings or threatened if they don't close their public spaces, Rustin is in their company.

Rustin is portrayed in the film by the esteemed, Emmy-winning actor Colman Domingo, for whom the activist has long been an icon. Domingo said, "Bayard seemed to have gotten his strength from his grandparents who raised him, Julia and Janifer Rustin, who were Quakers and very active. And they really helped him become who he was. Even when he came out to them at a young age, it was never met with any judgment. It was like, 'Well, that's who you are, and who you are is good.' So I think he learned those lessons early on in his life. I think that gave him strength and courage and fortitude to be exactly who he was at a time when the world was definitely saying, 'Temper that down.' It's the gift that he was given as a young person."

The anniversary of the abolition of slavery, the Emancipation Day of 1863, has not been the subject of sizable public commemorations in way over a century. But in December 1962, Rustin visited A. Philip Randolph, portrayed in the film by the Emmy-winning and much-revered actor Glynn Turman, and they discussed commemorating the 100th anniversary of the Emancipation Proclamation—a milestone little more than a month away. Randolph's dream of a march in Washington, D.C., came up, and Rustin in that moment was possessed of the desire to have Randolph see his dream realized.[7] In early 1963, Rustin began to approach civil rights organizations with the idea. In March 1963, Julian Bond, communications director of the Student Nonviolent Coordinating Committee (SNCC), told Rustin they were interested. SNCC was then led by John Lewis (later Congressman Lewis).[8] Next, James Farmer, national director of the Congress of Racial Equality (CORE), agreed to join. In May, Dr. King, president of the Southern Christian Leadership Conference (SCLC), added his organization.[9] After that, the goal was to recruit the most well-known civil rights leaders, who would round out the March leadership, known as the Big Six. One of the many striking moments in the film takes place when "Chief" Randolph and Rustin first suggest the idea of the March to the two remaining men.

Seated at the table with the others were Roy Wilkins, then the executive secretary of the National

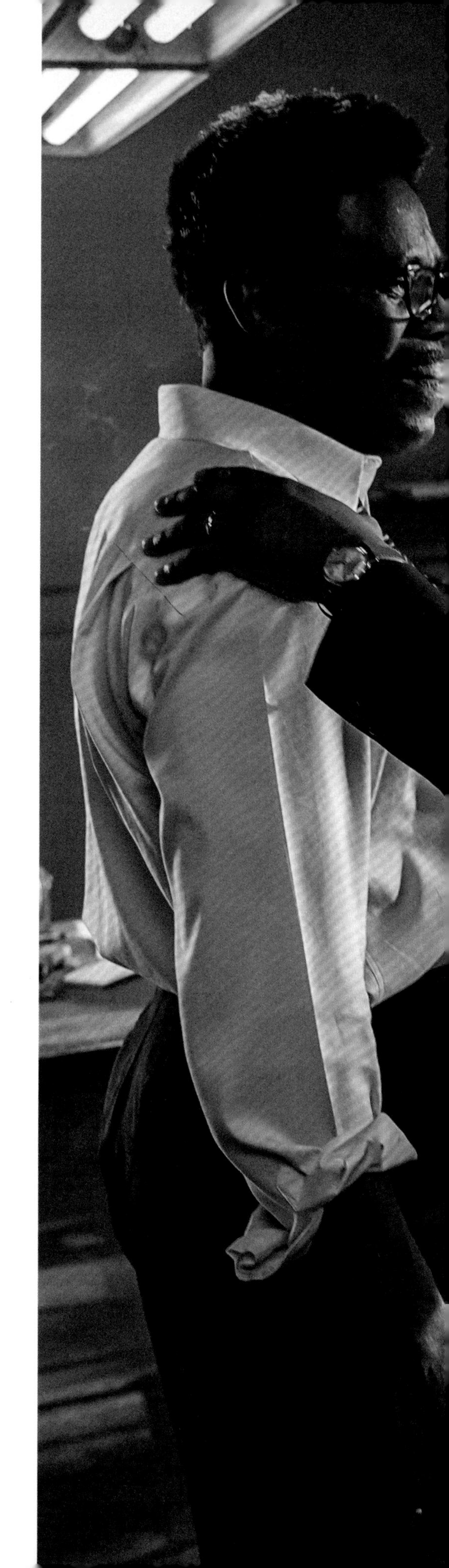

RUSTIN:

I'm the one that's been preaching passive resistance since before you were born.

Association for the Advancement of Colored People (NAACP), and Whitney Young Jr., then executive director of the National Urban League.[10] As we see in the film, it is immediately apparent to everyone present that, for various reasons, the March would have to happen very soon. The task is clearly daunting, especially when Rustin and Randolph say they are thinking they'd like 100,000 people to show up. What is most delightful is the twinkle in the eyes of Rustin and Randolph, the joy they are trying to contain as the others list the problems. As each difficulty is brought up, they listen and nod, yes, that will be tough. Smiles. The plan was in their heads; the issues had been numbered somewhere else before. Regardless of the real challenges raised, they know the others will not be able to resist. "The Chief," A. Philip Randolph, was named director, after an awkward refusal to have Rustin, who would do the work, seen as their lead organizer. The leaders agreed, under a bit of pressure, that only leaders of "civil rights groups"—eliminating a group like the National Council of Negro Women—could appear as the organizers of the event. The event known as the March on Washington was born.

Barely more than a month before the March, Congressman Adam Clayton Powell Jr., the most powerful Black person in the United States Congress, decided he wanted to be in the leadership, and with civil rights legislation under discussion in the U.S. Congress, he was included.[11] On August 28,1963, the smiling assurance of Rustin and Randolph was realized beyond even their confidence—250,000 people came to Washington, D.C.

Colman Domingo puts Rustin's frame of mind well. "I think that Bayard was like, 'Okay, you're not for me, but I'm for this—I'm for the movement. You don't have to like me, but you have to like what we're about in trying to bring people together...'That requires a lot of heartache and joy at the same time. Everything I know about Bayard Rustin was that he was a very joyful human being who loved life. And he wanted people to be responsible to and for each other as a country and across the world—all races, all creeds and religions. There is this mixture. Because you're fighting against a system, many systems, and all you care about is what's right and what's in the center—which is love, which is grace."

So some may say Bayard Rustin was ahead of his time, but he was only ahead of those of us who didn't know we were marching in his wake and empowered by his work. Everything felt right on time. Bayard Rustin feels more on time every week. The news shows people trying to turn back the clock to exactly those old days when hate could be a sign in any window denying the rights of others. *Rustin,* the film, is as timely as could be. It shows a man urging us that doing the most we can do is reward itself—such that at the end of our exertions we can look at our work and say, "Lord, I hope and pray they come today." As Rustin tells us in the film, "own your power."

RUSTIN:

Then they're going to have to fire me, because I will not resign. On the day that I was born black, I was also born a homosexual. They either believe in freedom and justice for all, or they do not.

DX-86-22

GRIOT OF CLAIMING IT & OWNING IT

GEORGE C. WOLFE, PRODUCER AND DIRECTOR

The acclaimed and transformative director and playwright George C. Wolfe has given us singularly memorable works in his esteemed career. A Directors Guild Award winner for *Lackawanna Blues,* Wolfe also directed the 2020 film adaptation of August Wilson's *Ma Rainey's Black Bottom,* which garnered five Academy Award nominations and two wins. A creative force in the world of theater, Wolfe has received 23 Tony nominations, with five wins for his work on *Angels in America* in 1993, *Bring in 'da Noise, Bring in 'da Funk* in 1996 and *Elaine Stritch at Liberty* in 2002. In 1995, the New York Landmarks Conservancy named him a "living landmark," and in 2013 he was inducted into the American Theater Hall of Fame.

In reflecting on his memory of the period in which Bayard Rustin was helping to shape southern resistance to segregation, Wolfe described his childhood introduction to Black citizenship. "I was a very, very young boy when all of the boycotts were happening in the '50s. Martin Luther King Jr. came to my hometown, Frankfort, Kentucky, for a march in 1964. My grandmother took me out of school, and I marched with her. All of that viscerally lives inside of my body. It's not this alien thing, but one of the things that was fascinating when I was doing research for an exhibition for the Center for Civil and Human Rights in Atlanta, some

“George Wolfe loves actors. He loves them, so he takes care of them. And he does that in a myriad of ways.”

AUDRA MCDONALD

to Refuse Service
to Anyone
We are
APPLE
PIE
60¢
with ice cream

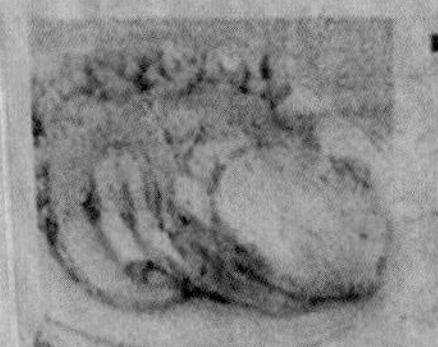
MEAT LOAF
DINNER
Choice of
$1.25
VEGETABLE SOUP
with crackers
75¢
TURKEY
DINNER
$1.25
Choice of beverage

MARCH ON WASHINGTON
FOR
JOBS & FREEDOM

SNCC
SNCC
MARCH ON WASHINGTON
FOR
JOBS & FREEDOM

years ago, was realizing, 'Oh my God, everybody was so young.' It was transformational because I remember them as adults. And it really, really informed my thinking about this film and casting the team of young people and how their open, available, smart faces became so crucial to the storytelling. And how important it is to capture that sense of being ready to take on the responsibility of helping to redefine America."

It is important that Wolfe is a southerner with such memories. It almost doesn't matter what age you are the first time you march down the main streets of your hometown with everybody you know and many you don't. The street, empty of traffic, filled with song, is lined by people stymied by the idea that you too are a citizen and can make known your needs and demands. It gives you power even when you are too young to know why they are staring in disbelief. It replenishes that sense of power with which we are born and felt the day we first walked, and may have forgotten by age six. And the insight of those marches diminishes the intended power of unjust practices such as poorly equipped schools, reluctant service in public places, stares, and denials meant to keep you shut out.

On both occasions in the film when Rustin steps onto a segregated bus, you feel something southerners knew well. The suffocating closeness of people, the low ceiling and heat, take the viewer far from the present moment and into a very different daily life remembered now only by elders. Wolfe's family may have done what mine did in trying to prevent unnecessary run-ins with what they called "second-class citizenship." Rustin's grandparents gave him something similar, such that the first time we see him board one of those buses, when he refuses to move to the back, he is conscious of giving a small child a lesson in the price of southern privilege. Those stifling moments were made that way by southerner George Wolfe, who perhaps remembered the feel of what King was talking about when he told us to break the grasp of that stale air in our lungs. One thing is for sure, Wolfe became one of those "young and so ferociously committed, focused, open, available and smart humans," so crucial to the storytelling in *Rustin*.

Producer Tonia Davis said that Wolfe came to the production more than prepared. "Not only did George C. Wolfe bring an incredible vision to the film from day one," she said, "but he also brought his incredible team with him. Mark Ricker, our production designer, who had worked with him on *Ma Rainey*, came back to do another tour. The work George and Mark did together on *Ma Rainey* was flawless and critically acclaimed, but also their working relationship was filled with trust and collaboration and a healthy amount of fun, too. George is a filmmaker in the truest sense of the word. He trusts his collaborators, particularly those he's worked with before."

"He was the right person for this story," said producer Mark Wright. "George digs deeper than just the facts on paper. And he is such a gifted director. While watching him work with actors, you see him use that same skill with which he massaged the script and the dialogue to massage performances. When actors show up you see he spent a lot of time rehearsing with everybody individually and collectively in scenes. Watching him push people gently and making sure that they felt safe to be vulnerable and to be themselves and to bring different parts of themselves to the role has just been magnificent. Everyone has their own style of directing—George's is about finding, uncovering, and honoring the truth."

"George Wolfe loves actors," said Audra McDonald. "He loves them, so he takes care of them. And he does that in a myriad of ways. He makes the space in which you're going to be working with him a safe space. He is a fierce advocate for actors. He's there to educate them and, at the same time, guide them to help them grow in the process of playing these characters. He makes these people three-dimensional because they were. So we understand that they have their flaws, their weaknesses, their strengths, and he let's you see all of it."

Colman Domingo spoke about George's approach as a director, fondly recalling their collaboration on the Academy Award–winning *Ma Rainey's Black Bottom*. "I'd auditioned for him before, but when I got the offer for *Ma Rainey's Black Bottom*, I thought, 'George C. Wolfe cast me?' And then we got to go on the journey of *Ma Rainey*. And to be honest, I didn't know that we would become as *trusting* of each other. There's such an openness with George. George is one of the smartest human beings walking this earth—he's brilliant. And he's got stories and ideas, and he challenges you to know something, to unknow something. He's playing with character and story like clay, and it's constantly evolving. And he's not married to one way. He's like, 'Oh, let's try that.' 'Let's throw that out.' 'Let's try that.' He's always excavating. And he's taught me how to do that and reminded me that that's part of the joy of how we create, how we dive deeper, how we let go and liberate ourselves for the work. I've learned a lot with George, and I'm so grateful."

George C. Wolfe explained how he took a detail-oriented approach to making sure the film was accurate and authentic to the period. "We have 857,000 meetings about how to do that, and it's an ongoing process. At one point when I was editing, I found myself for hours on end looking at the holes in young men's ears—nobody had earrings back in 1963. So, making sure all of that was plugged up. Every single detail. The lines in the street were not yellow, they were white. Everything is 1963 or 1942, because we sort of jump around briefly in time. So it's about making sure that every single detail puts you in the moment. And sometimes you cheat that a little bit, but by and large, it's very important that you get the details of history. It was their truth. It's what they were encountering and what they were overcoming.

"I remember at one point we were scouting locations in D.C., and the crew was standing around and we were talking about where we were going to park this, and do that, and all the details involved in shooting there. Then at one point, I said, 'It's taking all of us to capture this moment that this man did without cell phones, without anything. They built a machine. They built a human machine.' And when you think about that, it becomes even more of a miraculous phenomenon."

Asked about what he wanted to convey with the costumes, Wolfe said, "Well, one of the things that's really fascinating to me about the Civil Rights Movement was the phenomenon of TV and live coverage. The people in the movement were very savvy about image. They showed up for the sit-ins immaculately attired. When the cameras captured it and you saw these kids, in black-and-white, flawlessly groomed, and you saw a bunch of crazy people attacking them. Who looked like the smart, decent human beings, and who looked like the crazy people? Where I grew up, there's the person who you were inside your house, and then the second you step foot outside your front door, the whole world is watching you. The whole world wasn't, but that was the thought process—that as a young Black person, you represented the entire race in *every single thing* that you said or did. Everyone knew people judged them on sight, no conversation. What they did was all part of a campaign to transform America's stories."

Referring again to his youthful experiences in Kentucky in a community in action, he said, "It's why I do what I do. It's why I tell stories, be it in film or theater. It's just a sense to craft and celebrate the collective. What happens when passionate people come together, and they're focused on an idea. And I just love that phenomenon, and I love being a part of that phenomenon." Asked if he hopes that is what young activists of today take away from the film, Wolfe said, "Yes. The exact same thing. It's your country. It's yours. And if it's yours, you have to honor it. You have to clean it. You have to protect it. You have to do what you need to do in order to keep it alive and moving forward. It's your responsibility. Own it and claim it. You're smart and commanding. Take it and make it yours."

NEXT GENERATION DREAMERS

PRESIDENT BARACK AND MICHELLE OBAMA, EXECUTIVE PRODUCERS

"The moment I knew that Barack and Michelle Obama formed the production company after his presidency," said Colman Domingo, "I thought, 'Wow, that's a great way to make an impact in the world.' And the idea to be a part of their first narrative is just extraordinary. This story is important. This story matters. It says a lot about who they are by giving love and light to this film. I'll just say that this has been the most extraordinary time of my life to portray this man. It's like how John Lewis said, 'We want to get into some good trouble.' And I think we did."

In a conversation with George C. Wolfe, Michelle Obama remarked: "*Rustin* is an incredible reminder to young people about how complicated democracy can be. We all know about the March on Washington, but few know how it was organized, how the seats were filled, how space was made. It took years to get to this critical moment in our history, and there was a lot of backstory that happened along the way. There was a lot of drama, too—and that was natural given how big the movement for civil rights was. It just embraced so many people of different backgrounds, religions, identities, and viewpoints.

"One of my favorite parts of the movie is the way it emphasizes the power of gathering with people physically. That power is something I saw up close when Barack was running for office. Seeing all those like-minded people of different backgrounds and ethnicities standing shoulder to shoulder will always stay with me. I truly believe it's important to gather with people who you share values with as a way to prevent yourself from falling into isolation, anxiety, and fear. So I think this film serves as a reminder in building a movement, you're also building a community, too."

Mrs. Obama also spoke with George about the actors in *Rustin*, saying, "The power of these men and women. It just does my heart good to see this incredible cast on the screen doing what they do best. That's another reason why movies like this are important—because of all this talent that doesn't get an opportunity to be in lead roles, to tell the story in a broader way. Hats off to this amazing cast."

Marchers arrive at Union Station in Washington, D.C., for the March on Washington, 1963.

I WAS THERE

BRUCE COHEN, PRODUCER

Bruce Cohen, an Academy Award winner for best picture for *American Beauty,* has produced other highly acclaimed films, including the Academy Award–winning *Milk,* his first collaboration with one of *Rustin*'s screenwriters, Dustin Lance Black. Cohen recalled how he came to the film project. "I had originally gotten involved with the project when Dustin Lance Black brought me the screenplay. I had known about Bayard Rustin and his significance to the movement, and I also understood that many people didn't know Bayard or his story. So I was immediately intrigued and excited when Lance mentioned the idea of bringing this project to the screen. My first impressions when I read the script were what an extraordinarily powerful and beautiful and unique man Bayard was, and what an incredible contribution he made to history with the idea to do the March on Washington—the planning of that, its execution, and how important it would be to tell his story so that the world knows it."

Cohen was particularly excited about having Higher Ground and the Obamas involved. "Higher Ground was my first and dream choice to reintroduce Rustin and his historical significance to the world," he said. "To have the Obamas be a part of that will just solidify Rustin's importance and solidify the potential of the film to really change how people think about history. The fact that Higher Ground loved the script and that the Obamas wanted to be a part of that was just thrilling." Cohen added, "Bayard had an idea. He put this group together, and they had no clue at that time if they would be able to put on what would become the largest march in history. That was something that President Obama really highlighted to us in the script development. He said, 'You know, maybe it's easy for kids today to think 'Oh, just another march'—because they've seen the Women's March and all, and marches around gun control where hundreds of thousands of their generation came out.' But," Cohen recalled, "Obama said, 'When Bayard put on the March on Washington, he invented that.'

"I feel a deep kinship to Bayard Rustin. Throughout my career as a producer, my night job has been as a social activist fighting for many causes, including LGBTQ+ causes and racial equality. I relate to his passion for activism, and to get to play my small part to bring his story to the world is deeply moving and incredibly exciting. I previously produced *Milk*, a story about Harvey Milk, and there are some moving and important similarities, because Milk was also then a character in danger of being lost in history. So I feel that Bayard Rustin's name and legacy are going to survive, and our film will have played a role in that, which is as much as you can ask for as someone who works in the entertainment industry."

Cohen shared ties he sees between Rustin's time and today. "This film comments on contemporary issues in so many ways, largely because many of these same issues of racism and homophobia are still with us today. Some things have changed, and you see the great work of people like Rustin has moved things forward, but a lot has not changed. We had this very profound moment when we were first shooting in Washington, D.C. We were shooting footage of the Big Six organizers of the March walking toward the Lincoln Memorial. And the props and set-dressing people had re-created the protest signs that people were carrying in 1963. And we were all so struck because those issues, they're all still prevalent today."

WE MARCH FOR JOBS FOR ALL NOW!
WE MARCH FOR JOBS FOR ALL
DECENT HOUSING
FIRST BAPTIST CHURCH

ARRI

CHAPEL

RUSTIN
Cast & Crew 2021
RUSTIN

TONIA DAVIS, PRODUCER

"When we were starting Higher Ground, a lot of projects came over the transom," recalled Tonia Davis. "Barely by the time the Obamas had announced that they were going to have a company, there was already a flood of incoming submissions and scripts. Bruce Cohen, who is a producer I've always wanted to work with, called and said he had the perfect project to launch the company with. When he said that he had a movie about Bayard Rustin, we literally couldn't wait to read it. From that point forward, we knew we were going to get involved in this film one way or the other. George C. Wolfe was just coming on board, and we knew we had work to do before it could be green-lighted, and, of course, we had to bring Netflix into the project."

Asked why the immediate reaction on *Rustin* was yes, Davis said, "We're taught in schools that a few people, a few great men, created the world we live in today. But in fact, it's thousands of people, hundreds of thousands of people, who have given their lives and their energy tirelessly to create a more just world. So it feels like the right time to us at Higher Ground to lift up the unknown stories of some of the other heroes. People like those who showed up at the March, the people who organized it, those kids who worked tirelessly day in and day out in that sweltering summer of 1963. For me, as a gay woman, knowing that I am standing upon the shoulders of other queer people in history as we forge forward today is important. It is important to my bosses as well."

Making change is also much more possible, in Davis's view, if whole human beings are shown on the screen. "I think it's important to show love in all of its many forms. To show gay love, straight love, queer love, love of any kind, familial love, the love between Bayard and Martin, not romantic but the brotherly love and the mentoring love—that's just as important in this film as the love between Bayard and Elias or Bayard and Tom. What happens in this film is that we show Bayard as a complete human being. Not just a homosexual man, not just an organizer, not just a Quaker, not just a pacifist, but we try to show his whole self and that's exactly what it took for him to bring the energy, passion, commitment to making the incredible March on Washington happen."

She added that whatever encouragement the film provides for people to get involved in change is welcome. "The need for organizing for progress has never been greater than today. When we think about what's going on in this country, we need to always remember that the power of the collective is going to outweigh the power of the individual. We, as citizens, can always do more."

MARK R. WRIGHT, EXECUTIVE PRODUCER

"I had been generally aware of Bayard Rustin just by my own research. When I found out that there was a script about his life, I immediately began to wonder: How do you begin to encapsulate the magnitude of this man's contributions to society, to the Civil Rights Movement, to the LGBTQ+ community, by way of his existence and advocacy? I'm just so amazed by the work that has been done to get this story to where it is. And focusing on his participation in the March on Washington, I thought, was incredibly smart, just because it directly ties his contributions to a very tangible moment in time that people can latch on to, reflect on, and use to anchor him in history.

"I hope that people look at this story and see it as a reflection of our time today and see it as an honest and critical portrayal of history. Ideally, people will look at it and think we can't just overlook a figure like Bayard Rustin because of his sexuality. He was, after all, the reason the March on Washington came to be. It was due to his brilliant mind, his being a logistician and a person who could see people's talent and put them in the place where they could be their best selves and be most useful to the task. I think it will give us pause when we think about whose stories we're telling when we reflect on the times today and who gets to be the hero. Often, we like to sanitize history, pick the pieces that make us most comfortable. But I think it's when we're uncomfortable that we become the best versions of ourselves."

MARCH on WASHINGTON for JOBS
and FREEDOM
BUTTONS 25¢
MARCH ON WASHINGTON
FOR
JOBS & FREEDOM
AUGUST 28, 1963

RUSTIN'S SCRIBES

JULIAN BREECE AND DUSTIN LANCE BLACK, SCREENWRITERS

Widely celebrated for bringing awareness to the legacy of LGBTQ+ activist Harvey Milk in his Academy Award–winning screenplay for *Milk*, Dustin Lance Black ignited the spark for getting a film about Rustin off the ground.

Julian Breece spoke fondly about the early days of their collaboration: "When I heard Dustin Lance Black was looking to make a film about the life of Bayard Rustin, I leapt at the opportunity. Bayard had been a hero of mine since I was a child. I'd even studied his work in the anti-war and Black freedom rights movements in college. Lance read my work, we met and the next day I got the call that he'd wanted to bring me on to write the screenplay. I give him credit for hiring a Black queer writer to help tell Bayard's story."

Black explained his inspiration for the film: "In 2009, I stepped away from filmmaking for a time to focus my energy on equality work, helping build a U.S. Supreme Court case for marriage equality and a March on Washington for LGBTQ rights. What became clear to me then was that many of the fragile coalitions of minorities and equality-minded Americans that had existed before had fractured, leaving all parties with less power, influence and hope. So I turned my attention to the lessons of one of my greatest inspirations: Bayard Rustin. Bayard's ability to see past ego to the greater good to be found in locking arms with people of different races, backgrounds, religions, and experiences, and his extraordinary ability to unify these often divided people in order to win power and progress guided and fueled my equality work into the 2010s. It seemed clear to me that if we were to make progress for minorities in this country again we would have to bridge our deep divisions and work together again. Bayard was my guiding light."

The incredible story of Bayard Rustin and his involvement with the March on Washington went through a compelling journey to the big screen. Co-writer Julian Breece reflected upon his experience of seeing the film for the first time and what he hopes audiences will gain from it: "I attended a screening of George's early cut of *Rustin* and got chills as I realized just how timely and urgent the story is. Years ago, when I wrote

WORK WITH YOUTH
WASHINGTON. D.C

the screenplay, my hope was that it would become a film that shined a brighter light on Bayard's story—the story of a man who'd been deemed an outcast in this country only to become the same man whose March helped rescue us from an era of violence and racial intolerance. Back then I couldn't have imagined that the film would come out exactly sixty years after the March on Washington, at a time when our country's history seems to be repeating. Now my hope is that audiences will not only see Bayard's work on the March as a victory in the fight for black liberation, but also as a road map for change and healing that's just as powerful today as it was then."

The screenplay of *Rustin* focuses on the short, very dynamic few months that Bayard Rustin had in which to put together a march he hoped 100,000 people would attend. Black discusses the tight time frame of the film's main action: "I believe we can get to know anyone fully in a film by meeting them in an extraordinary circumstance that tests their sense of self, their courage, their bedrock ideas and principles. There is no need for a birth-to-death biopic to know someone. And, frankly, such films are generally dull. So what moment could be better to meet Bayard in than depicting a landmark historical event that people think they understand but don't. A moment as iconic as the 1963 March on Washington. The truth is that most don't know how and why the March came about. And most certainly don't know that an extraordinary civil rights fighter who was openly gay in a time when that was a crime and considered a mental illness built this extraordinary, iconic moment for the world to come together in the name of equality and justice."

Over the course of the project, Breece and Black did extensive research, including interviewing key players in Bayard Rustin's circle, such as Walter Naegle, Rachelle Horowitz, Dorie Ladner, Joyce Ladner, and Eleanor Holmes Norton, all of whom offered a wealth of knowledge that proved critical in shaping the script. Breece said, "Meeting Bayard's friends and family was one of the most rewarding experiences of my life. Speaking to Bayard's partner, Walter Naegle, deepened my understanding of the private Bayard, the Bayard most people never knew. Those conversations stayed with me, and in the ten years since, Walter has become one of my most treasured friends."

Black said, "I began my own research meeting with the surviving people who knew Bayard in the 1950s and '60s and many others who helped build the March." Once Black felt he had Bayard's story and character in his bones, he did his rewrite using the new knowledge, characters, and themes he had uncovered. Black said, "What inspired me most in the research wasn't Bayard's political genius. I had long known about that. What I found now was a deeply emotional, sexual, loving, musical, life-loving man. A complete human being with flaws and temptations. For me, Bayard's personal life was as moving and illuminating as his political and organizational brilliance. And so I felt that if I could meaningfully rewrite a screenplay that was as sensual and glittering as the Bayard I'd come to know, we had a shot at an extraordinary biopic about this extraordinary man."

Asked about the film's themes of inclusivity and exclusion, and the contradictions in the characters' practice, Breece said: "If writing about Bayard's life taught me anything, it's that being Black and queer in America makes us the ultimate outsider-insiders. We possess the same double-consciousness that W. E. B. Dubois described as the feeling of being distinctly American while feeling forced to perceive oneself through a lens of whiteness. Our queerness adds yet another lens to that toolbox, giving us access to a unique, bird's-eye view of the social order in this country and our place within it. For Bayard, that dynamic way of perceiving the world proved to be his superpower and a curse. Bayard's strategic genius didn't spring only from his years of experience as an organizer or formal study. It came from his deep empathy for humanity and his ability to see people's fears and needs without judgment. With that clear view of the field, Bayard was able to launch missiles into the central nerve of those systems of exclusion. Unfortunately, like many geniuses, Bayard's gift also left him feeling isolated from the people around him. In the film, his journey is to regard himself with the same preternatural empathy and grace he extended to so many others, and to finally embrace even the most maligned pieces of his identity and see himself as whole."

Black said, "I am thrilled the film now exists. My hope is that people will find it and realize once again that locking arms with people who are very different, people who may have suffered more or less in today's still-unequal world, will begin to rebuild the necessary coalitions Bayard worked so hard to create, and that new leaders will grow from Bayard's example, so that we may push that pendulum of progress forward again. I believe Bayard Rustin's story is that powerful."

ELEANOR
How big?

BAYARD
100,000 people.

CHARLENE
Is he for real?

BAYARD
A massive two day demonstration with the power to shut down the White House, and Capitol Hill, made up of angelic troublemakers such as yourselves, with actions so bold and inspiring, the execution will demand all groups draw tightly together and become one. So let's hear 'em--

23 A SEAMLESS SMASH TO LATER-- 23

There are now FIFTEEN KIDS, hereafter known as THE TEAM, sitting on the couch/floor/windowsill. There are cartons of take-out scattered about, and cups of Deli Coffee are being passed around. BAYARD MOVES ABOUT THE ROOM, like a coach amping-up his team before the big game.

BAYARD
All your ideas. Talk! Shout! Take command!

ELEANOR
What if we flood the offices of every member of the House and Senate, with delegates from church, labor, civil rights--

Bayard gestures, 'keep going."

ELEANOR (CONT'D)
...And in such numbers, the Legislative branch will cease to function.

BAYARD
(offering a marker)
"Flood Legislative Offices." Write it on the wall.

As Eleanor does--

THE MAKER OF GOOD TROUBLE

COLMAN DOMINGO AS BAYARD RUSTIN

"When I knew that I was going to play this figure," said Colman Domingo on preparing for the role of Rustin, "I thought that I had been given such a tremendous opportunity to shed a light on one of my personal heroes, someone that I discovered many years ago outside of high school and college, and finally as a performer. There was a theater production about Rustin in which I took over for an actor, and that was the first time I learned about him. So, when this opportunity came, I took a deeper dive into his legacy and his history. I wanted to truly make him as complex and human and interesting as the man himself. It's an extraordinary honor.

"I embarked on about five months of research. I read biographies. I watched documentaries like *Brother Outsider: The Life of Bayard Rustin*. Looked at anything I could get my hands on, especially interviews with Rustin and people who were around him, like Eleanor Holmes [Norton] and Rachelle Horowitz. He was an original in every single way, and someone who didn't put limitations

MUSTE:

Every day we agree to surrender that which makes us different, so that together we might forge a more humane world.

RUSTIN:

I can't surrender my differences. The world wont't let me. And even if I could, I wouldn't want to. Not today.

on himself and thought outside of the box, even with the way he grew his hair out, especially in the 1950s and early '60s.

"I needed all the textures that make someone human. So that's what I leaned into for Bayard Rustin. For instance, I know that Bayard didn't have a lot of bass in his voice when he spoke most of the time. I really wanted to make sure that there was an element of Bayard in his speaking that was a bit elevated, leaning somewhat towards that mid-Atlantic standard he crafted. And yet I had to keep it very grounded. I didn't want it to be about the voice, but it's an element."

Leaning in also included accommodating other physical details as much as possible. "Through production design, costume design, hair, everyone got behind all of this detailed work," said Domingo, "to make sure that it all just lived and breathed and there was a full human being, every detail was there. I have prosthetic teeth. I noticed the way he smoked and the way he would hold his hands. I just tried to put these images into my body. And so I did a lot of work with that to make sure that hopefully I could just trust that it would come out in the scene somewhere, the way he stood, the way he would pull up his belt, the way he would lay, the way his clothes fell on him.

"I study the whole person, not just what they're saying and what the script's saying. I studied images of what was in his home. Who is this person who has all these plants in their apartment, all this different furniture and things from around the world? All that stuff informs how you play him. So, even the scene when I cook for Ella Baker, we discussed in detail. 'What will he cook?' I said, 'I think he'll cook Indian food.' I said that would be a comfort to him because of the time he spent in India. We did all that little stuff which I felt freed him and let him be full and human.

Bottom: Bayard Rustin speaking at the Madison Square Garden rally against the war in Vietnam, 1965.

"I think the time to take Bayard out of the shadows of American history has been coming for a very long time. And I'm so grateful that our producers, Netflix, and Barack and Michelle Obama's company, Higher Ground, believe that his story is profound and will resonate with today's audiences. It's important. Every time I turn around, I can tell someone I'm playing Bayard Rustin, and they're like, 'Who?' And it's shocking, because this man was so significant to everyone's struggle, you know? After this film comes out, I would like to never hear, 'Who was Bayard Rustin?'"

Producer Bruce Cohen is thrilled with Domingo's work in the role. "Colman Domingo is the right actor to play Bayard Rustin in so many ways, but he's only exceeded those expectations with his mind-blowingly brilliant performance bringing Rustin to life," said Cohen. "He looks like Bayard. He sounds like Bayard, but without doing any type of imitation. One of the things that was a dream of ours was that we would find an openly LGBTQ+ actor to play Bayard Rustin, an openly LGBTQ+ activist. Part of the reason for the film and what audiences will learn was how completely rare and unusual it was to be out in 1963 as a gay man. Bayard was a huge trailblazer for that, and so we really wanted an out actor. Colman was, in that respect as well, the perfect choice. And I think that will really excite audiences and add to the authenticity of what we are doing.

"For a long time, Blackness and queerness were amplified separately. There was no intersectionality. In many ways, I think, *Rustin* is going to do something different. You're not just getting an openly gay man but you're also getting his ideas, his organizational skills. You're getting the fullness of this man. It's not limited to his queerness, and it's not limited to his Blackness. The intersectionality makes a full human being. And, hopefully, we're in a place where there will be more projects green-lit that live in that space."

CP826
CHARTER
WASHINGTON D.C.
WASHINGTON D.C.
GM

RUSTIN:

A massive two-day demonstration with the power to shut down the White House, and Capitol Hill, made up of angelic troublemakers such as yourselves, with actions so bold and inspiring the execution will demand all groups draw tightly together and become one.

TRAINS
PLANES
NEW YORK CITY
TRAINS
PLANES
BUSES
Overcome

TELEPHONE

DRINK
10 15

APPLE
60¢
DINNER
Choice of beverage
$1.25

NON-
EGYPT
SUDAN
GHANA
GUINEA
CAMEROON
RLEM
ARE
REPA
RECRU
WAR! WAR! YES, A HELL OF A WAR
MESSY MISSISSIPPI
FROM HARLEM SQUARE
DICK GREGORY
JACKIE ROBINSON
HARLEM SQUARE
SPONSORED BY
MISSISSIPPI RELIEF COMMITTEE
HUMAN RIGHTS POLITICAL ASSO.
DICK GREGORY will be at the APOLLO THEATRE
IN THE EVENT OF BAD WEATHER MEETING WILL BE HELD AT ABYSSINIAN
BAPTIST CHURCH, 132 West 138th Street, New York City
NEGRO MAKERS OF HISTORY

PEOPLES
AFRICAN CHIEFS OF STATES
CONGO
SOMALIA
NIGERIA
EAST NIGERIA
HEADQUARTERS
TO AFRICA
FREEDOM COUNCIL IN AMERICA
HERE!
WHITE MAN'S GOD
This Can't Be Him Because He Has the Wrong Hair
& SHOE
SHOE REPAIRS TAKEN
WASHINGTON for JOBS
and FREEDOM
BUTTONS
CANNOT
IGNORE
WHAT WE
REALLY
WANT TO

MARCH
NOW
JOIN THE

unteer
HER

ICONS OF THE MARCH

CIVIL RIGHTS LEADERS

When the idea of calling 100,000 Americans to the National Mall took hold between Bayard Rustin and A. Philip Randolph, they knew it would take the forces of all the best-known civil rights groups to make it possible. Bringing them all into one discussion put three generations of Black activists at the table. The first to express support were the very youngest, the Student Nonviolent Coordinating Committee (SNCC), headed up by John Lewis, who continued his activism until his last days, during which he protested the murder of George Floyd.

The oldest figures in the group, who came to be known that year as the Big Six (who were in fact at least seven), were born at the turn of the twentieth century, between 1889 and 1908. A. Philip Randolph, the NAACP's Roy Wilkins (the self-appointed leader of the Big Six), and Congressman Adam Clayton Powell Jr. all had in common, due to their age, the living memory of the slave system in their family life. Rustin, who was born in 1912, also had the living memory of slavery in his grandparents' home and, though he grew up in the North, also had daily familiarity with institutional segregation.

James Farmer of CORE and Whitney Young of the Urban League were born in the 1920s, and were people who benefited directly from parents who were educated and taught at historically Black colleges and universities (HBCUs). Their families' education early in the century made them part of the intelligentsia and leadership in their communities.

All these men abhorred segregation but the eldest, Randolph, and the youngest—Young, Farmer, Lewis, and King—had grown up with institutional segregation. Young left Kentucky at age 20, Farmer left Texas at 18, and by 1963, they were in their early 40s. Dr. King was 34 years old. He had first left the South at 19, so one may imagine that all of them saw in the 23-year-old Lewis a reflection they recognized—but Lewis was a man who had stayed in the South for the fight for justice, in part because he had seen

Some of the leaders of the March on Washington in front of the Lincoln Memorial, August 28, 1963. Bottom row, from left: Whitney Young, Cleveland Robinson, A. Philip Randolph, Dr. Martin Luther King Jr. and Roy Wilkins. Top row, from left: Matthew Ahmann, Rabbi Joachim Prinz, John Lewis, Reverend Eugene Carson Blake, Floyd B. McKissick and Walter Reuther.

King speak. King's grandfather had been a sharecropper but was able to get to Atlanta and attend Morehouse to answer his calling to the ministry. Following his father-in-law's death, the elder King became the dynamic minister of Ebenezer Baptist Church, building a congregation several thousand strong. King's background resembled those of the older men in terms of the assets and safety nets of the middle-class Black community, and we see him struggle in moments when they exert the power of class solidarity and their personal fame to bend him to their will. In the film, Rustin aptly terms their influence as "the suffocating chains of Negro respectability."

Lewis did not grow up with a pulpit to inherit. His family were sharecroppers who repeatedly warned him not to get in "trouble"—which meant very simply not invoking the wrath of whites in any way. Lewis mentioned in an essay written just before his death that he was a 15-year-old in Alabama when 14-year-old Emmett Till was murdered in Mississippi.[12] He refers to Till as his George Floyd, and in fact it had been a devastating event that helped shape most of the young activists working on the March. Many of Lewis's peers in the movement, especially in SNCC, have recalled that defining moment in interviews. Lewis's desire to be a minister drove him to get the education that, in turn, gave birth to Lewis the activist. Meeting King inspired Lewis to learn to face the wrath of a mob with nonviolence, which he did many times. He was quite shocked late in life to learn that his ancestors had voted in Alabama during Reconstruction, and risked their lives getting into "good trouble."

The life experiences of these men who left home to make change were clearly empowering for them. They all had a similar confidence in winning in the face of opposition as they formed their organizations to "fight the power." Fortunately, for all of us seeing *Rustin*, we get to see each in his own style of gamely taking on the task (as well as each other) and joyfully doing the impossible. As Rustin says, ready to take on all comers, "They either believe in justice and freedom for all, or they do not."

Leaders of the March on Washington stand united at the front of the March.

WE DEMAND
AN END TO POLICE BRUTALITY NOW!
WE MARCH TOGETHER
CATHOLIC JEWS PROTESTANT
FOR DIGNITY AND BROTHERHOOD OF ALL MEN UNDER GOD
NOW!
WE MARCH FOR
INTEGRATED SCHOOLS NOW!
UAW SAYS:
GOD of Justice
GOD of Power
CAN AMERICA DENY FREEDOM IN THIS HOUR?
FREEDOM FOR Every American
WE MARCH FOR
JOBS FOR ALL NOW!
WE MARCH FOR
JOBS FOR ALL DECENT PAY NOW!
DECENT HOUSING

GLYNN TURMAN AS ASA PHILIP RANDOLPH

In *Rustin,* Glynn Turman, an award-winning actor and director, and one of the deans of Black actors, plays a man who was the dean of Black activists in the twentieth century and the legendary force behind the 1963 March on Washington for Jobs and Freedom. Turman, who began his professional career as a young teen appearing in the original production of Lorraine Hansberry's *Raisin in the Sun,* steps into the role of a man who dreamt of being an actor.

Asa Philip Randolph (1889-1979) is most well-known for three activism victories. In 1925, he formed the Brotherhood of Sleeping Car Porters, the powerful union of Black railroad workers that not only fought for fair labor practices for those men but inspired the formation of other Black labor organizations, including domestic-worker groups. He called off his first March on Washington in 1941 when he won an end to discrimination in the war industries, and in 1948 his other protests led to the desegregation of U.S. armed forces. In 1963, while planning the March, Randolph was mourning the death four months earlier of his wife, Lucille, to whom he was devoted over a 49-year marriage.

Turman reflected on playing the eminent organizer: "Mr. Randolph was a very powerful and influential man during the times portrayed in our film. He was a man who was used to taking on the establishment big time. He caused quite a ruckus for a couple of presidents. He was a man of big ideas and was able to get things done. He was quite a gentleman, but he had an inner core that was pretty tough." On the period portrayed in the film, Turman said, "I feel a kinship with Randolph and Rustin, first because I know those times, certainly the '60s. That was the world I grew up and was maturing in—that was my time. I know the landscape that these men walked in. I know the police baton, and 'You can't eat here, you can't sit there, you can't live here.'"

Producer Bruce Cohen said, "George immediately knew that for A. Philip Randolph, Glynn Turman would be the perfect casting, and he's turned out to be just that. Glynn is such a phenomenal actor. He has done so many great performances in so many great films, including, most recently, *Ma Rainey* for George. It's been such a great pleasure and honor to get to see Glynn work."

Turman was asked about preparing for the role. "Well, quite a bit of research is available nowadays," he said. "I just went back and started reading things. And a very helpful thing was the time we spent in Washington, D.C. I was able to go to the National Museum of African American History and Culture. And there, it was all laid out. I was able to really take in everything we had previously researched, but there it was bigger than life."

Turman also spoke of the work of matching the image to the man. "Toni-Leslie James has just done a wonderful job in putting all of us not only in the period but also looking good in the period. That prepared me, along with the photos I've seen which showed how he took care of himself and how he presented himself to the world. That was an era when men and women, especially in the struggle, were people who had to talk to presidents. They were people who had to talk to leaders of the nation, and they had to present themselves accordingly."

Turman describes his hopes for the film in terms of audiences relating it to the current state of the nation. "Audiences should take away how fragile and precious our democracy is. How it should be guarded and defended. How American we are as a people. And when I say as a people, I mean all of the people are uniquely American because of these ideas that we have tried to define so that we all have space in this great America. And if you come away with that, then we've done our job."

Portrait of civil rights activist A. Philip Randolph.

A. Philip Randolph and Bayard Rustin on the cover of *Life* magazine, September 1963.

MARCH ON WASHINGTON
FOR
JOBS & FREEDOM
AUGUST 28, 1963
MARCH ON WASHINGTON
FOR
JOBS & FREEDOM
AUGUST 28, 1963
March on Washington
For Jobs and Freedom
Wednesday, August 28, 1963
PLATFORM
GUEST

JEFFREY WRIGHT AS CONGRESSMAN ADAM CLAYTON POWELL JR.

Adam Clayton Powell Jr. (1908-72) grew up in a privileged household and earned degrees from Colgate University and Columbia University. The year he was born, his father was asked to run the Abyssinian Baptist Church and turned it into the church with the largest Protestant congregation in the country. It has the unique history of being founded in 1808 in Lower Manhattan by Ethiopian seamen who objected to segregated seating in New York churches. The younger Powell ran crusades for jobs and affordable housing and rent strikes in the 1930s. He took over the pulpit in 1937 and, in the 1940s, led boycotts of businesses on 125th Street, where most businesses did not hire Blacks. Often referred to as flamboyant, he was a fiery speaker, who combined thorough understanding of the Bible with exposition that was both erudite and hip, politically incisive and humorous. He was a man who famously married a glamorous Black showgirl, Isabel Washington, then a chorine at the Cotton Club, and then married Hazel Scott (and others later), the famous jazz pianist and singer. He was what reporters called "good copy," and the church was a powerful base for Powell that sent him to the U.S. Congress. In the 1950s, Powell began to chafe at the rising prominence of Roy Wilkins, a sometime ally, and especially at the rise of King and all the attention received by the southern Civil Rights Movement underway. He also made negative remarks about King having Rustin as a mentor. This may have been both jealousy and prejudice, as Powell had made some unsavory remarks referring to "sexual degeneracy" earlier in the decade. Again, he was good copy for reporters.[13] In 1959 and 1960, he quietly used sexual innuendo to threaten King and get him to abandon a protest plan for the Democratic National Convention, and in the process alarmed King into having no contact with Rustin. Adam, as everyone called him, was used to being adored, but Congress acquainted him with being despised. He used his power to irritate them for fun and cripple them when he could. After hearings to exclude him, the House of Representatives refused to seat him in 1967 for various violations, but he returned only to lose his seat in 1970. In 1963, Powell was the most powerful Black person to ever sit in the U.S. Congress and was working to pass equal-pay legislation, bills for the War on Poverty, and was soon to pass legislation establishing Medicaid.

What did Jeffrey Wright, winner of a Tony, an Emmy, an AFI, and a Golden Globe award, think about this charismatic Powell, who, depending on who you asked, was adored, feared, despised, or envied? "Adam Clayton Powell Jr. is a fairly complicated character. He was the first Black congressman from the Northeast, elected in 1945, and the first to represent the district that includes most of Harlem. He was a long-serving congressman and had a good deal of power, particularly during the Lyndon Johnson presidency. And he was also a minister. So he was a massive character, not only in Harlem during the Civil Rights Movement but he was in some ways the most powerful Black man in America. He was a dynamic leader, but also a performer. He had charisma and a dynamism about him that was a blend of Washington and Hollywood. He was just a super-magnetic figure, with an outsized ego. But at the same time, you know, he was committed to serious progressive politics on behalf of working people, on behalf of Black people in his constituency and the larger citizenry of the United States. He was a serious, serious agitator within the halls of power, on behalf of the marginalized and underserved people of this country. He was a singular guy, committed deeply to the cause and to the people, but also deeply committed to himself and his own ego. So, an interesting man."

Bruce Cohen remembers Wright being imagined for the part. "Jeffrey Wright is clearly one of the great actors of his generation. And when you're doing a film like this, you dream to have Jeffrey Wright bringing one of the characters to life. Jeffrey and George have a long history of doing incredible work together. So it was easy for George to realize that the person to bring the flamboyant character of Adam Clayton Powell to life was Jeffrey Wright. And fortunately for all of us, and fortunately for the audience, Jeffrey agreed that he would step into the very large, very fancy shoes of Adam Clayton Powell for us."

Wright himself was taken with the talents of the others in the cast. "George has assembled a room of great actors. And what's wonderful about that is that you really only show up and bring your thing to the table, and you bounce it off what everyone else is bringing to the table. When you have assembled a group of actors like this, it just makes it easier because everyone is feeding off one another and no one's dropping the ball and everyone's just keeping the energy and the ideas and the moments in the air at the table. And it's good fun. There's an athleticism to it in a way. If you watch a great soccer team or basketball team move the ball around the court or field, and you see the way they're synchronized and the way they move and anticipate one another, that's what happens when you assemble a room full of wonderful actors, and you have a good story in front of them. It's that same type of dynamic. And ultimately that's what makes the scene and the story sing—the ways in which we work together."

"Oh, boy," Mark Wright recalled, "when Jeffrey Wright showed up on set the first day in his Adam Clayton Powell complete hair and makeup, everybody was just like, 'Damn, he looks just like this man.' Powell was a complex man. I think if you look at the complexities of who he was as a political leader, and as a figure of the Civil Rights Movement, there are many different opinions that live on as part of his legacy. And I think to capture the essence of that complexity—a man who saw his work in one way and that history might see differently, depending on where you fall—you need somebody who is able to dig into themselves and find complexity and humanity, and not just play this role as a kind of villain. Jeffrey Wright is that actor in every sense of the word. He has the chops. He's able to pull from different parts of himself. In the middle of a scene, he will keep digging and keep trying to find the truth and to find that moment that is going to be surprising, that is going to really bring new layers and depth to the scene."

Wright's idea of a welcome reception for the film is that it inspire others. "I hope people take home an appreciation for this history and for those who led the work that was done that affects all of us to this day, people like Bayard Rustin. If we look at the ways in which they went about their work, they left a playbook. I hope people take away a sense of possibility that in even the most challenging times, with the right leadership and the right ideas and the right work, progress can be built. The people who forged this history, like Bayard Rustin, Dr. King, and Rosa Parks, are examples to all of us of what is possible. So, I think we take away from this a bit of hope at a time we could use that."

“In the middle of a scene, he will keep digging and keep trying to find the truth and to find that moment that is going to be surprising, that is going to really bring new layers and depth to the scene.”

MARK R. WRIGHT

Following pages: (*right*) Portrait of Adam Clayton Powell Jr. in 1946.

CHRIS ROCK AS ROY WILKINS

One of the country's most beloved comedians and winner of multiple Grammy and Primetime Emmy awards, Chris Rock comes to the role of Roy Wilkins with an acute sense of the political, as shown in his comedy, acting, and directing. Roy Wilkins was also a household name in his time, the most often quoted spokesman for civil rights issues.

After getting his B.A. from the University of Minnesota, Wilkins (1901-81) began his career as a newspaperman, becoming editor of the *Kansas City Call*, a legendary Black paper founded in 1919. He became assistant secretary of the National Association for the Advancement of Colored People (NAACP) in 1931, and edited *The Crisis*, after W. E. B. Du Bois's departure in 1934. In 1950, Wilkins joined A. Philip Randolph and Arnold Aronson, a leader of the National Jewish Community Relations Advisory Council, in founding the Leadership Conference on Civil Rights. In 1955 he became head of NAACP and came to be identified more with court cases than protests, even though the court actions were the work of the NAACP Legal Defense and Educational Fund, a separate organization founded by Thurgood Marshall in 1940.These developments were part of Wilkins's legacy as well, aiding the view of him as too cautious in a time of growing militancy.

"When we were looking at pictures of Roy Wilkins," producer Bruce Cohen recalled, "George said, 'You know, he looks a little like Chris Rock.' That was what gave us the initial idea, and it gave us the courage to reach out to Chris and see if it was something that he would be interested in. Chris has a great passion for activism and social justice and was very familiar with Bayard Rustin and Roy Wilkins and their importance to the history of our country. He was excited about the chance to work with George and to work on this movie, and we're so happy and fortunate that he wanted to come along."

Rock shared his enthusiasm for being part of the project. "George is one of the best directors I've ever worked with. He's really into your motivation. You know exactly why you are in every scene. You know exactly why you're saying every word. And George is really into preparation—we rehearsed for about two months before we started shooting."

Mark Wright added, "We were very excited to work with Chris. He's been doing more and more dramatic work lately. And it was very exciting to have the opportunity to work with him, and to see him with this cast. He is a tried-and-true and trained comedian and comedic actor. So it's exciting to see him continue to push himself and stretch at this point in his career, and it's an honor to have him do that in this movie."

Opposite: Roy Wilkins speaking at a union convention, 1958.

AML AMEEN AS REV. MARTIN LUTHER KING JR.

Rev. Martin Luther King Jr. (1929-68) had returned to Atlanta from Montgomery at the time of the March on Washington. He moved to run the SCLC and was co-pastor of Ebenezer Baptist Church with his father. His sojourn as minister of the Dexter Avenue Baptist Church in Montgomery had made him famous. This was an outcome that would not have been predicted when the newly married minister had taken the job after finishing his Ph.D. King had graduated from Morehouse College (having started at age 15), had then gone to Crozer Theological Seminary for a divinity degree, and then Boston University. When he and Coretta King arrived in Montgomery, the Black community was already engaged in protesting segregation. This new minister, who was neither friend nor foe to any of the local organizing factions, proved an irresistible pick as the voice of the yearlong mobilization set off by the arrest of Rosa Parks. By 1963, King's life had been threatened for over 10 years, including the bombing of his Alabama home. He had been involved in several now-famous nonviolent protest actions, including the difficult Albany, Georgia, movement and protests in Birmingham, famously involving the hosing and beating of schoolchildren. By 1963, King was being spied on by the FBI and had embraced Gandhi's nonviolent approach to making change. This last development was due in great part to having become close friends with Rustin, who, by then, had been advising him for seven years.

The next year, 1964, King received the Nobel Peace Prize, and he continued to organize and respond to calls for support from activists around the country. He was murdered in Memphis, Tennessee, in 1968 answering one of those calls, supporting striking public-works sanitation employees. Days later, this tragic event helped spur the passage of the Civil Rights Act of 1968. The awards and honorary degrees he received are too numerous to list here, but several stand out: President Jimmy Carter awarded him the Presidential Medal of Freedom in 1977, a national holiday was declared in his name in 1983 by President Ronald Reagan, and a Congressional Gold Medal was named in 2004.

The gifted British actor Aml Ameen had the unique challenge of portraying Dr. King as a young minister assigned to his first church and making the transition during the film to becoming the storied King known across the world. Ameen was struck by the task of making those shifts from scenes as the young King to scenes a few years later, and "seeing how he's changed," after becoming the living embodiment of the Black movement for justice. Early on in Alabama, Ameen said, "King is the young, very smart, confident orator, but he's not quite that man yet....Martin is a really charismatic figure, and he's very funny. He's got that wink in his eye. And I was really interested in capturing that. And then years later, he's lost Rustin, and you can feel the weight of the world more."

"Casting Dr. King was a daunting task," said Bruce Cohen, "because he is such an iconic figure. He's so well known in history. The 'I Have a Dream' speech, which is at the end of our film, is legendary. And he is also well-known by being represented in film and television across the years. So to find an actor who, on one hand, looks and feels like the historic MLK, but on the other hand is bringing something completely new and fresh and exciting to the role, might have seemed impossible—but we found Aml Ameen, and he's done exactly that. When we shot him giving the 'I Have a Dream' speech, people were just stunned. After the first take, there was just this moment where we felt like Dr. King was back with us. We felt like he was there on the set. And I got chills then, and I get a chill now thinking about it."

"I had a transformative experience," said Ameen of that same moment, "in the sense of really understanding the idea that Martin and the men and women of that time were pushing forward was the power of the collective to change consciousness." On playing the young King on the day they shot the "I Have a Dream Speech," he said: "It's a very powerful moment. I would say that it's beyond words and comprehension. You become deeply honored and thankful and wonder why, and you just go with God."

Asked about working with Wolfe, Ameen said, "George is the type of director who keeps you—instead of thinking about the magnitude of the moment—just remembering this: We're all human beings with particular gifts, and back then, the moment met these people, and they used their gifts to create history. So,I love George as a director. I think he's earned the titles of griot and genius. Those are words you can certainly attach to his name."

"We wanted somebody who resembled MLK," said producer Mark Wright. "And we wanted somebody who would disappear in the role. I mean, MLK is such an epic figure, and you didn't want somebody who, when you cast them, would not be able to get past who they are as an actor or as a personality. And Aml brought all those things—the familiarity, the chops, and the ability to be able to disappear and not overshadow this titanic figure but also bring his humanity, bring the depth and layers to him."

WASHINGTON
FOR
& FREEDOM

MARTIN (ON TV):

Mr. Rustin is one of the most moral, one of the most decent human beings I have ever known. He is as committed to American democracy as any current elected official, and would fight to protect the rights of all, including those who would use the power of their positions to deny him his. I am proud to call him friend, and cannot think of a finer person to lead us in Washington, D.C.

Without warning, Bayard's emotions rush to the surface: tears, anger, frustration, hurt. Dr. Anna gently PLACES HER HAND AGAINST HIS BACK *while he cries. And then just as abruptly, Bayard wipes his eyes and smiles. He's ready and feels finally free.*

Following pages: (left) Dr. Martin Luther King Jr. delivers his "I Have a Dream" speech during the March on Washington, 1963.

MARCH
FOR
JOBS & FREEDOM
AUGUST

THE MOVEMENT'S SECRET WEAPONS

WOMEN ORGANIZERS ON THE GROUND

In *Rustin,* CCH Pounder, as Dr. Anna Hedgeman, holds up the adjournment of one of the last meetings before the March and, in doing so, halts the commission of an injury meant to shut down Bayard Rustin's role as the strategic and organizing center of the massive event. (One might add that the move to shun Rustin comes after he has done most of the work.) Hedgeman raises a grievance: the invisibility of women activists on the stage of the March. She reads a list of the excluded—women known already as the driving forces of powerful movements all over the country. She should have included herself as well, but we see her say these words: "I look at this program and I do not see one woman's name. Not Ella Baker or Diane Nash. Not Dorothy Height, Gloria Richardson, Mrs. Prince Estella Lee, Myrlie Evers, Rosa Parks, or Daisy Bates." Except for SNCC organizer Diane Nash, who was John Lewis's age, most of these women were peers of the Big Six, and Hedgeman was of Randolph's generation. Their names constitute a group of some of the most legendary organizers and inspiring leaders in twentieth-century activism. Lifting weight in their class is not easily done.

To play Hedgeman and Ella Baker, Bruce Cohen said, "We wanted the Who's Who of actors today to be a part of this film, and we feel like we've really accomplished that between Audra McDonald playing Ella Baker, CCH Pounder playing Dr. Anna Hedgeman, and Da'Vine Joy Randolph playing Mahalia Jackson. Those are just three examples of these extraordinary historical female figures being brought to incredible life by some of the great actors of our generation." Unknown to most people, for instance, was a vital role Mahalia Jackson played beyond singing, when during the speech she reminded her old friend King to talk about his dream. The actors in the film playing these women took very seriously their historical place in the shadows of the March.

Crowd of women cheering at a meeting in Montgomery, Alabama, during the ongoing bus boycott, 1956.

AUDRA MCDONALD AS ELLA BAKER

Ella Josephine "Jo" Baker (1903-86) was born in Norfolk, Virginia, and grew up in North Carolina. Her family lived on farmland her grandparents had bought as freedpeople from the plantation where they had been enslaved. Baker graduated from Shaw University as valedictorian in 1927 and moved to New York, where she began a career of activism, starting with collective Black economic development with the Young Negroes Cooperative League in 1930. She worked as a field secretary with the NAACP starting in 1940 and as director of branches from 1943 to 1946. By 1955, she was raising money for the historic Montgomery Bus Boycott and, by 1957, had moved to Atlanta to help Rev. King organize the newly formed SCLC. There she also ran a voter-registration campaign, Crusade for Citizenship, a forerunner of the kind of mobilization done there today by Stacey Abrams.[14]

After students at North Carolina Agricultural & Technical College sat in at a "Whites-Only" lunch counter in Greensboro in early 1960, Baker left the SCLC and organized a meeting of college protest leaders, and SNCC was formed on a basis of nonviolent direct action. Among young activists, Baker was given the nickname "Fundi," a Swahili word for one who teaches a craft to a younger generation. Her most famous saying, which many of us young people heard then, perhaps while stuffing envelopes in a SNCC office somewhere, was often quoted: "My theory is, strong people don't need strong leaders."

Producer Bruce Cohen was thrilled with the choice of Audra McDonald, the six-time Tony Award winner, who also has two Grammy Awards and an Emmy, to play Ella Baker. "Audra McDonald, if I may have a little fanboy moment, is just one of my favorite actresses of all time. I will stop what I am doing, and I will run, not walk, to see anything Audra is in. Getting to see her onstage is always a thrilling and phenomenally memorable moment. The same with her extraordinary appearances in film and television. If Audra McDonald is in a project, you know that it's going to be something special and magical. So I was thrilled when George wanted her to be Ella Baker and even more thrilled when Audra agreed to come and bring Ella to life."

At the first sight of her in *Rustin,* one wonders, Who is this woman? Simply dressed, plainspoken, getting right in Bayard's face to listen and then shake him out of his misgivings or hesitations. On preparing to play Baker, McDonald said: "There's a lot of historical documentation and there's a lot of footage where she gives her own narrative, and I think that is always a very powerful thing when you don't really get to interview the person.

There's a danger in trying to imitate someone. Instead, it's more about capturing their essence, the truth of who they were and what they wanted and what they were trying to accomplish. And what Ella is trying to accomplish in this film is to facilitate the bringing together of minds that she feels will make the movement have more energy and get the March into that powerful place, helping to mend fences, all of that. For me, it was just about understanding who she was, understanding her truth, and then using that truth to facilitate what she wants to happen in this particular moment in history. You know, there is the story of Bayard Rustin and his journey to this moment in civil rights history that could have been like a textbook. It could have been told in that way that would have been boring. But you want to understand that at the end of the day these are all still just human beings moving about in space, trying to get their needs, as well as the *need* of the greater good, taken care of. And within that, forgive the expression, but people aren't just black-and-white. There are so many shades of gray to who people are. George explores all of that. He makes these people three-dimensional because they were. So we understand that they have their flaws, they have their weaknesses, they have their strengths, and he lets you see all of it. He lets it be messy because life is messy and history is messy. And that, I think, brings an immediacy to it, especially for an audience of this new generation coming up who can see and maybe resonate with them. They can recognize themselves in these people, instead of them just being like people who are on postage stamps.

"There's a part of me sadly that thinks if those organizers were to think ahead about now, they may have thought we'd be past all of that. But at the same time, they would see that there are people out there still using a lot of the techniques that they used, the grassroots organizing which comes from Ella Baker's message and theory that it can't just be from the top down with some charismatic leaders."

George C. Wolfe said of McDonald, "I worked with her on Broadway, and she and I had known each other for a long time. But that show was the first time we worked together, and there's such a purity of focus about the work. There's a purity of focus about the task at hand, doing the job, and that just struck me, and so I thought, 'She's the perfect Ella Baker.' There's that same sense that I felt about Baker—'Now this must be done, and so let me do it.' And not a bunch of floaty ego crap. It's do the job, do the job, and she's magical."

Following pages: (right) Ella Baker in Washington, D.C., 1941.

CCH POUNDER AS DR. ANNA A. HEDGEMAN

Anna Arnold Hedgeman (1899-1990) was born in Marshalltown, Iowa, and grew up in Anoka, Minnesota, where her family became the first African American residents of the town. She was the first Black graduate of Hamline University and then taught at Rust College, an HBCU in Holly Springs, Mississippi. In 1924, she began a 14-year career with the YWCA, acting as executive director of Ys (then designated as "colored" Ys in the North and the South) in Springfield, Ohio; Jersey City, New Jersey; Philadelphia; and Harlem and Brooklyn in New York City. In 1944, she became executive director of the National Committee for a Fair Employment Practices Commission, and starting in 1957, she served in the cabinet of New York City mayor Robert F. Wagner Jr., the first Black woman to hold such a post. In her work on the March on Washington, Hedgeman, working through the National Council of Churches, brought 40,000 participants to the event.

Acclaimed actress CCH Pounder, who has received numerous honors for her work, including multiple Emmy nominations, creates a presence as Hedgeman that literally can silence a room full of healthy egos in dispute. What did Pounder think about Anna Hedgeman? "Dr. Hedgeman is like a thousand other women who worked tirelessly on a project—who have the brains and the moxie to get the work done and are most unaccustomed to being praised for it. I really tried very hard not to make her feel like a hero but as a cog in the wheel of progress. What Mr. Rustin and Dr. Hedgeman did in their time is remarkable. It's heroic and it's unsung. I've received recognition and praise in my life because in our times of change and love, tolerance, acceptance, things have opened up for folks like me. So, what a privilege it is to bring her to the screen. Hopefully the audience will see just a tiny bit of what so many women like Dr. Hedgeman had to go through."

Pounder was most taken by being at the shoot on the National Mall. "The heat on the day that we were there," she recalled, "was a reminder that the people who actually did it had no tents to run to, to cool off with the AC blowing in—just buckets of ice, maybe. When shooting, we were in unrelenting heat, so I imagine the sun and the concrete must've been incredible on the actual day. And what I felt I don't think matches what it must've been like for them, the electric excitement that they must've had during the real march. I've already received all the privileges that they provided for me on that day. They are the flag bearers for that single day that changed the course of history, and as always there is an inner story of pride, determination, and sheer chutzpah to get that job done knowing that many in your own household are against you—that makes a hero."

Civil rights activist, educator, and writer Anna Arnold Hedgeman.

DR. ANNA A. HEDGEMAN:
Bayard, when I was a girl, every night my father would ask, "Have you been useful today?" I'm more than certain that has been true for you most of your life. But today my child... Today.

HEDGEMAN'S LIST

To best honor Anna Hedgeman's indignation with the Big Six, for excluding women activists from speaking at a march for equality and freedom, it's important to lift up those she wanted recognized. We know how fragile their place in history has become when we hear of recent efforts to edit American history books, such that even Rosa Parks, once a household name, is being subjected to erasure proposals. Hedgeman's list includes Ella Baker and six women whose names were then revered in communities in which they worked across the country. In fact, Baker knew or was friends with nearly everyone on this list.[15] This is almost predictable due to the breadth of her work, but it is also likely due to the fact that women in leadership anywhere were the exception, not the rule. Pressure from Hedgeman resulted in one minute being allotted to Myrlie Evers, and when it turned out Evers could not make it, the slot was given to Daisy Bates.[16] I have added Fannie Lou Hamer, who was that summer recovering from a vicious jail beating and yet registering what turned out to be nearly 80,000 Black votes in Mississippi that fall.

Annie Devine, Fannie Lou Hamer, and Victoria Gray outside the United States Capitol, 1965.

DAISY BATES
(1914-99)

was a civil rights activist and newspaper publisher in Arkansas, who ran the on-the-ground organization of the 1957 school integration by the Little Rock Nine, the first integration drive after the *Brown v. Board of Education* decision in 1954.

DIANE NASH
(1938-)

was the lead organizer of the Nashville sit-ins, when she was a Fisk University student, and was jailed in that movement. She became a founder of SNCC in 1960, and organized volunteers for the CORE Freedom Rides, which began in 1961. She was appointed in 1963 by President John F. Kennedy to a national committee to promote civil rights legislation, which became the Civil Rights Act of 1964. She and James Bevel started the Selma-to-Montgomery marches, which gave us the Voting Rights Act of 1965.

DOROTHY HEIGHT

(1912-2010)

was president of the National Council of Negro Women from 1958 to 1990, for which she was generally assumed to be a member of the national civil rights leadership, if not considered an equal by the men in such positions. She also worked for the YWCA from the 1930s to the 1970s, heading up programs at "colored" YWCAs in three cities and serving on its national board. In the year of the March on Washington, she was leading the desegregation of community YWCAs.

FANNIE LOU HAMER

(1917-77)

was a legendary leader in voter registration and women's rights in Mississippi. She also helped SCLC voter-registration efforts. As a result of this work, she was subjected to many of the worst terrors of white supremacy in Mississippi. She planned SNCC's Freedom Summer in Mississippi and was a co-founder of the Mississippi Freedom Democratic Party (MFDP), which sought to be seated at the Democratic National Convention in 1964. She turned out that event by speaking so fiercely that President Lyndon Johnson had the TV networks interrupt her speech.

GLORIA RICHARDSON

(1922-2021)

led the intense but successful three-year-long fight by the Cambridge Nonviolent Action Committee (CNAC) for desegregation in Cambridge, Maryland. She was arrested and daily faced the National Guard that filled the city for two years. At the time of the March, the movement was moving toward conclusion but still on. She was present but not seated with other leaders.

PRINCE ESTELLA LEE

(1917-2015)

was widow of activist Herbert Lee, who was murdered in 1961 in broad daylight in Liberty, Mississippi, by a Mississippi state representative, for aiding SNCC activist Robert Moses in a voter-registration drive.

MYRLIE EVERS

(1933-)

At the time of the March, Evers had just become the widow of Medgar Evers, field secretary of the NAACP in Mississippi. He was murdered June 12 in Jackson by a member of the White Citizens Council. She worked with her husband on voter registration and desegregation of public businesses and of the University of Mississippi.

ROSA PARKS

(1913-2005)

was an NAACP activist in Alabama starting in 1943 and, during that decade, also worked on several cases seeking justice for Black women who had been raped in that state. She became the most famous of the women responsible for the Montgomery Bus Boycott and was a veteran of other justice movements. She was present at the March but not seated on the podium.

BRINGING RUSTIN TO THE BIG SCREEN

STORIES FROM THE FILM'S ARTISANS

"At one point," George C. Wolfe said, "we were filming certain scenes at the Lincoln Memorial in August in Washington, D.C., which, lest we forget, was once a swamp. It was 100 degrees, and by the time the heat hit the marble of the Lincoln Memorial, we were working in 120 degrees. And then there is this archival footage that's just extraordinary, but only a finite amount of it was colorized—which was amazing—but a lot of it was in black-and-white. So we were just going in and exploring it and trying to use what we shot. I think we had about 500 extras. In sort of combing through that which was filmed, that which we had, with visual effects and all that stuff, it became challenging but, in some respects, a lot of fun and it was really fascinating colorizing the archival."

Cinematographer Tobias A. Schliessler further explained this task: "When we discussed whether we should try to match the look of the movie to the archival footage, we decided against it, as there was only a small amount of archival shot towards the end and we didn't want to degrade the majority of the film to match that look. Instead, we slowly started manipulating a couple of the shots before and after the archival ones for a smoother transition."

"There was this one shot," said Wolfe, "which I love beyond existence: There is a group of women who have just gotten off a bus in 1963, in this archival footage, and they all have curlers in their hair because they're going to look fabulous for this march and they're going to wait till the last second before they take these curlers out of their hair. There's so much in that—the vanity, the pride, their 'I'm ready to do it, I'm ready to do it.' There's so much embodied in that and you just see it. And then some of the women with the hats. There's so much storytelling, so much pride, and so much sophistication and attitude in how people are dressed, and it's just lovely to see."

PHILLY PRODUCTION CREW

FOCUS -
CL 50.0mm
BAT 13.9V
A216 C001
MEDIA 0:26 h
TC 15:58:47:03

TOBIAS SCHLIESSLER, DIRECTOR OF PHOTOGRAPHY

"Tobias Schliessler, who had been George's cinematographer on *Ma Rainey,*" said producer Tonia Davis, "came back to join us, as did Shelley Ziegler, our first assistant director. So we had the same key crew members all working together fairly flawlessly back in the city of Pittsburgh, where they had done *Ma Rainey* together so well just a few years ago. Tobias's work is exceptional. It's exacting. It's specific. It is moody. It's imbued with a sense of life and love and light. He understands George's vision and he understands it through the lens of a camera, and to have their collaboration, again, on this film feels incredibly lucky."

Schliessler was asked what drew him to this project. "I worked with director George C. Wolfe on *Ma Rainey's Black Bottom* a couple of years prior and had one of my favorite experiences shooting a movie. When he approached me to do *Rustin,* I knew immediately I wanted to collaborate with him again, especially on a film with such historical importance. Beyond the fact that it was an amazing project, working for Barack and Michelle Obama was an opportunity I could not pass up. Their passion and ability to bring stories like this to life are so important to our society, and I'm excited to see what films they make in the future. I am also very grateful to work with Netflix again, as they have been incredibly supportive of my career and all the projects we've done together. I love that they collaborate with companies like Higher Ground Productions and are passionate about making movies that matter. My hope is that *Rustin* inspires every person who sees it to be a peaceful, nonviolent advocate against the racial and sexual discrimination that is far too prevalent in our world today."

Schliessler discussed what it was like to shoot the March on Washington and capture both the epic scope of the event and the more intimate moments: "After our initial location scout to the Lincoln Memorial and the Washington Monument, it became very clear that shooting the scenes for the March was going to be our biggest challenge. The steps to the memorial are extremely limited for filming, crew, and equipment. You also cannot stop access for public visitors or hold them back from walking through the shots while filming anywhere on the Washington Mall. Minimal lighting and grip equipment are permitted but by far not enough to control the frame or light for any kind of continuity. Due to these reasons, we had no choice but to shoot Bayard's meetings with Chief Wells,

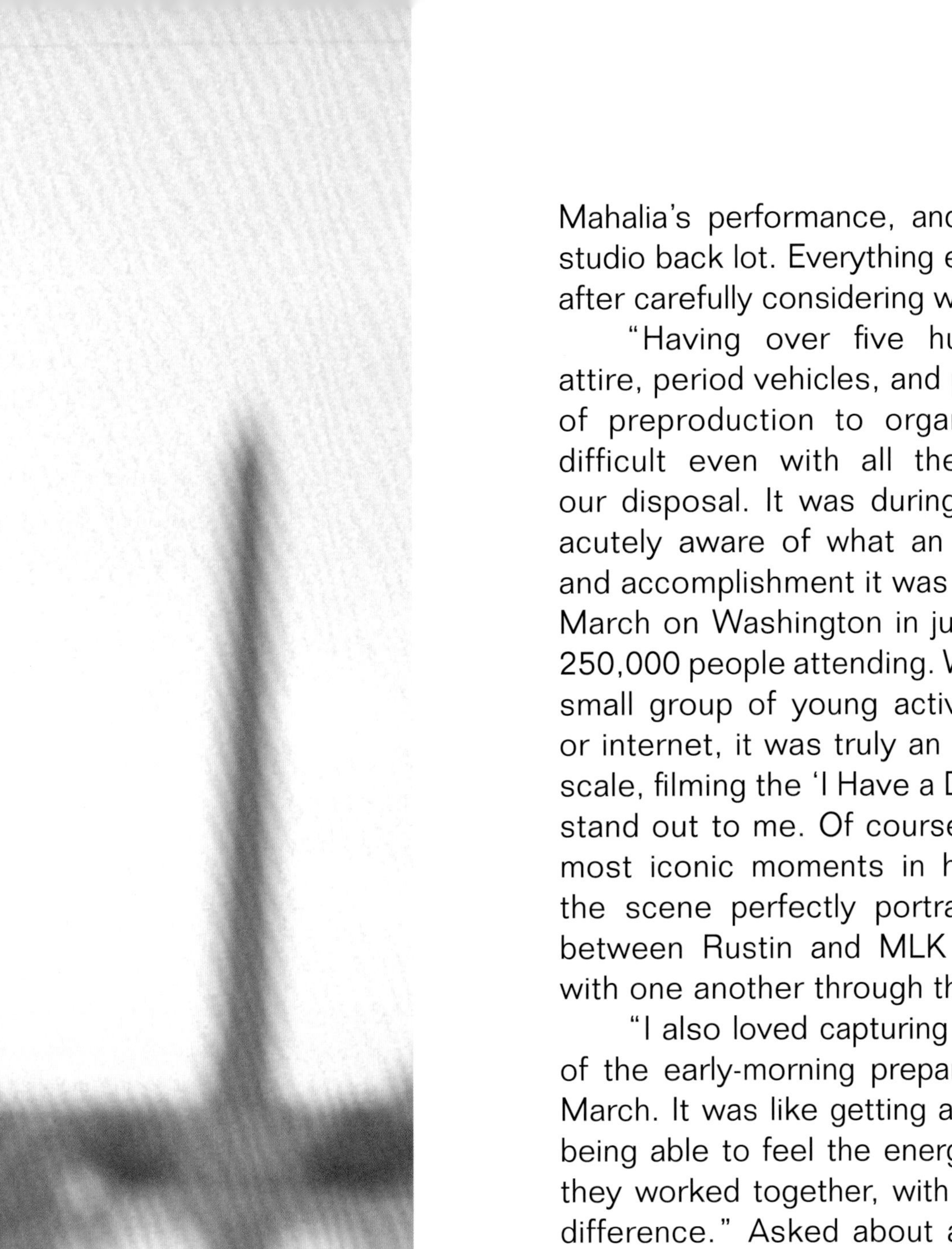

Mahalia's performance, and Dr. King's speech on a studio back lot. Everything else was done on location, after carefully considering what would be possible.

"Having over five hundred extras in period attire, period vehicles, and period props took months of preproduction to organize and was extremely difficult even with all the modern technology at our disposal. It was during this time that I became acutely aware of what an unbelievable undertaking and accomplishment it was for Rustin to organize the March on Washington in just over two months, with 250,000 people attending. With only the help of a very small group of young activists, and no cell phones or internet, it was truly an amazing feat. On a grand scale, filming the 'I Have a Dream' speech will always stand out to me. Of course, because it's one of the most iconic moments in history, but also because the scene perfectly portrays the deep connection between Rustin and MLK as they exchange looks with one another through the crowd.

"I also loved capturing the more intimate scenes of the early-morning preparations on the day of the March. It was like getting a glimpse back in time and being able to feel the energy of all the volunteers as they worked together, with every individual making a difference." Asked about a moment in the film that stands out for him, Schliessler mentioned a scene in King's Atlanta home, when Rustin is "waiting for Dr. King to arrive and to convince him to join his movement. He is in the small kitchen singing with Coretta Scott King and her children, 'This little light of mine, I am going to let it shine…' During the song, Martin arrives and watches as Rustin interacts with his family. It's a very intimate scene that beautifully illustrates Bayard's loving relationship with King and his family."

Working with Wolfe also had an impact on his work: "I love working and collaborating with George. He is what every cinematographer looks for in a director—someone with a clear vision, extensive knowledge of the material, and the utmost respect for the craft of cinematography. After every take, he checked in with me and ensured I had everything I needed on my end, which made working with him feel like a true partnership. During the early days of prep, we visited real locations in New York and Washington, and George would share his vast knowledge of African American history and the importance of the scenes we were to portray. This helped me understand the focus of the story and how we could properly tell it with the camera.

"George, the production designer Mark Ricker, and I all shared mood boards and images during preproduction, and we were able to establish the desired look for the movie early on. Having worked with both George and Mark on *Ma Rainey's Black Bottom*, this process felt very synergistic. One of the many strengths George possesses as a director is not only nurturing incredible performances from the actors but also the ability to block and choreograph the scenes in a way that is most beneficial for the camera. He likes to do this planning at least an hour before call, when the set is quiet and he can do this work undisturbed. We would then discuss the camera angles, movements, lens sizes, and so forth with our camera operators and first assistant cameras, to make the best choices to bring George's vision to life. This is the part I love most about filmmaking—collaborating with the director, the cast, and an amazing crew. There's a unique camaraderie formed on film sets that's hard to describe, but something I'm continuously grateful for.

"It was important for both George and me that the audience feel completely immersed in the film without being distracted by an aesthetic that felt too 'period' or overly stylized. We let the color tones of the sets, costumes, makeup, and hair define the era, while keeping our lighting classic and natural. We used vintage lenses and added a slight grain to the footage for a bit of 1960s character, but always made sure camera and lighting decisions were based on what would best serve the story.

"A major theme that influenced the lighting choices was that of Rustin's sexuality and living as a gay man in the 1960s. Having to literally hide in the shadows of society, George wanted to utilize lighting to help convey this feeling. This motivation helped me shape not only what we see on camera but also what we don't see, which was equally important."

MARK RICKER, PRODUCTION DESIGNER

Producer Tonia Davis was pleased when she heard Wolfe was bringing Mark Ricker on to the team, praising his work on *Ma Rainey's Black Bottom*. "When we first knew that we were shooting in Pittsburgh, Mark already had an idea of exactly which street corner we should shoot at, exactly what building we should cover, and exactly what we needed to build onstage to make sure the veracity of the film was complete."

Colman Domingo, who also appreciated Ricker's work from *Ma Rainey*, was still surprised by the design work for *Rustin*: "Mark is masterful. I love the world that he creates because it's truly so detailed. Like, we shot at this interior, in a bar, and I actually thought, 'Oh, is this a real bar?' No, it was just a space that had nothing in it, and he transformed it. It looks like a world, like it was truly honest and real. There was no lie in the room. And then when I walked outside and saw the cars and other shops, I couldn't figure out what was real and what wasn't real, which is the key to a great production designer. I thought, 'Has that always been here? Is that the way the street looks usually in the day?' No, we created all that. I just couldn't believe it. It really is magic what production designers do, and Mark is truly one of the best."

Actor Johnny Ramey, who portrays Elias Taylor, was stunned by the same bar: "I mean, walking in on the first day in the bar scene and seeing how it was all constructed from scratch, and seeing the background talent who were dressed to fit the environment… you walk in and, like, instantly you're transported into this bar that's been there for ages. You don't have to think about acting. You just be, and that is the biggest gift to give an actor, to walk in and just breathe."

Ricker said Harlem was a "specific challenge" on the film. "We needed a specific street where the March headquarters existed, and that just does not exist here. But in the way that we always do this in movies, particularly in my department, you find bits and pieces and you create just enough. You can discuss set extensions, which we're doing to a degree in this film. But Harlem, Harlem is very specific. And the most specific

CIVIL RIGHTS
PLUS
FULL
EMPLOYMENT
EQUALS
FREEDOM

MARCH ON WASHINGTON
FOR
JOBS & FREEDOM
AUGUST 28, 1963
ON WASHINGTON FOR JOBS AND FREEDOM AUGUST 28, 1963

DEF 3
ABC 2
1
TUV 8
WXY 9
0 OPERATOR
HOLD
SPARE
Editorial
Adver-tising
Circu-lation
Printing

THE ELBE LINE
MADE IN U.S.A.
INSERT TITLE CARD INTO CORNERS
NEW YORK—NEW HAVEN—HARTFORD—
WORCESTER—SPRINGFIELD—BOSTON
13
EASTERN
GREYHOUND
BUS
TIME
TABLES
JANUARY 3, 1963
SPRINGFIELD
WORCESTER
BOSTON
NON-STOP
TIME TABLES
BUFFALO
ALBANY
BUFFALO
ROCHESTER
BUFFALO
SYRACUSE
BINGHAMTON
ALBANY
EASTERN
GREYHOUND
EFFECTIVE OCTOBER 27, 1957

challenge for me on the project, I think, was the March headquarters. It's just a simple building, nothing special about it, but it sits on a block. In the script, we walk through a front door. We're on a first floor, a second floor, a third floor, which we built as stage sets. But we're also in a courtyard behind the building. We're also on the rooftop of the building. In Pittsburgh, that block doesn't exist. So the façade was one thing. The courtyard was a completely different location that we had to build sets in to create. I found two houses that offered enough architecture that we could then build a third side, and a bit of a fourth side so we felt some distance. Then there was a rooftop. My point being that, when it all comes together in the movie, it'll just feel like one building. Of course, because it's split over six or so completely different spots that all had to have a continuity of space and texture and what we would see out the windows, such that we would see the same thing in the rear of the courtyard, and on the rooftop, it was just a puzzle to figure out. I hope that we did a good job.

"But it's all in the details. The details of Bayard's life were so specific in his apartment. He was a bit of an eccentric. He traveled a lot. He had a taste for antiques and collectibles that he would get in Europe and then would later barter over with antiques dealers in New York. One of the challenges was how to pay homage to his interests and eccentricities without going over the top. I think we hit a good balance with showing what interested him to the degree that when I was speaking with Walter [Naegle] in his apartment, it struck me that there was no sofa. I said, 'Did he ever have a sofa? I mean, there's not a sofa here. There's not a sofa in the research.' I said it was almost like he was more drawn to the meaning of the furniture than the comfort of the furniture. He had a lot of throne chairs and ecclesiastic chairs. And Walter said that was exactly right. He sort of didn't want people lingering around too much. So you just take a detail like that, talk to the director, figure out what's going to work for the film, and go from there."

Chelsea
ONE HOUR
CLEANERS

CIVIL RIGHTS NOW!
DEMAND ACTION ON: JOBS
JOIN THE
: THE RIGHT TO VOTE
FREEDOM MARCH: DESEGREGATED SCHOOLS
WE PETITION FOR: FAIR HOUSING
WE WANT REFORM FROM: THE PRESIDENT
WRITE LETTERS TO: CONGRESS
U.S. CONGRESSIONAL DEMS CLUB:
ATTORNEY GENERAL

THE HOUSE OF COMMON SENSE
HOME OF PROPER PROPAGANDA
WORLD HISTORY
BOOK OUTLET ON
000.000.000
(TWO BILLION)
RICANS AND NON-WHITE PEOPLES
WASHINGTON BUSINESS INSTITUTE
HARLEM SQUARE
REPATRIATION HEADQUARTERS
BACK TO AFRICA MOVEMENT
RECRUITING
JORDAN
LL BOOKS
MAGAZINES
NIC S SHOE STORE
& SHOE REPAIR
Coca-Cola
LUNCHEONETTE
AL's LUNCHEONETTE
MARIE'S
Beauty Lounge
AMERICAN

CLUB 27
BAR

“You walk in and, like, instantly you’re transported into this bar that’s been there for ages. You don’t have to think about acting. You just be, and that is the biggest gift to give an actor, to walk in and just breathe.”

JOHNNY RAMEY

BRANFORD MARSALIS, COMPOSER

"George Wolfe called me and said, 'I'm doing a new movie called *Rustin*. Do you want to do the music?'" recalled Marsalis. "And I said yes. As a composer, at the start of a project, I don't know the actors or the on-screen vision. I just get a script. When you read a script, it's natural to create visual images in your mind, but that's your personal version of the story. I don't write music for my version of the story. My job really comes at the end of the process. Once I can see the scenes, that's when the music comes. I enjoy writing for films. I enjoy the process—it feeds a different side of my brain and I like that."

Wolfe commented on doing a third film collaboration with Marsalis: "One of the things that's really glorious about working with Branford is, in addition to being an incredibly gifted musician and an incredibly gifted composer, he's a musicologist and he understands. More than understands—he just knows. I knew I wanted a sort of jazz quartet driving us through New York City because the sound would instantly put us in early-'60s New York. And music in the Civil Rights Movement was so crucial, and a lot of that was springing forth from the Southern Baptist tradition, but Bayard being this anomaly, I wanted something that felt New York and sharp and cerebral and visceral all at the exact same time. And so that was the sound that I was looking for. And I would call him up with a question and I'd go, 'I'm looking for somebody who was a combination of this, this, this, and this.' And then like two hours later, I'd get six samples. And he doesn't have to go digging for it—he knows it. You can just have the conversation, he does the work, and it comes back different and magical and wonderful."

Marsalis contrasted the *Rustin* work with their last collaboration, *Ma Rainey's Black Bottom*: "I had to do a lot more audio research for *Ma Rainey* because I was not as familiar with the sound of music in the '20s and '30s. But there is a lot more musical variety in *Rustin*. I was able to write some scenes that had more orchestral parts—string orchestras with brass—that wouldn't have worked very well in *Ma Rainey*. But the research that I did for *Ma Rainey* bleeds over into everything I'm doing now, so they're related in the larger sense of the word. I learn something from every project I do, so each time there is something that's a little better."

"George is a big jazz-head, and he said, 'I want jazz.' And I said, 'Great, we'll get a big band.' So I started writing with big band in mind. The opening scene is a good example. It's kind of like this montage between the points of view of Martin Luther King and Adam Clayton Powell and Bayard Rustin. I looked at that scene for ten days, and nothing seemed to work. The one thing that worked in the end was a driving big band—great jazz has propulsion.

"I didn't set out to create a '60s soundtrack," said Marsalis. "I have to write music that creates a certain kind of emotional tension for the scene that's going on. But there were times when some of the '60s music really did work. There was a funky jazz sound happening at the time. Small jazz combos were playing funky soulful stuff. There's a cool scene in the movie that's based on a factual story about planning a fundraiser for the March on Washington where the '60s sound really worked. Stevie Wonder recorded a song called 'Fingertips' when he was twelve years old. He sang some lyrics, played the harmonica, and was backed by a big band with jazz luminaries like Coleman Hawkins, but what people remember is Little Stevie. I recorded a big band to go underneath that fundraiser scene, inspired by the 'Fingertips' arrangement they had done, even though you don't hear a lot of it in the recording. That part is similar to the true '60s sound.

"This is the kind of movie that's right up my alley. You *could* just do one thing. You could use a string orchestra, or you could use a jazz band, or a small group, but it would really be ineffective for this movie. It's great to have *all* those colors at different points in the movie, depending on the subject matter and the energy that the actors are bringing. Some people will see this film and be inspired or surprised. Many probably don't know who Bayard Rustin is. My hope is that one outcome of the movie will be more discussion about his contributions to both the Civil Rights Movement and the Gay Rights Movement."

LYRIC W/ MELODY
1
I N'ER DIDS'T DREAM E-
-E - - - VER THE DAY SU - - CH HEAVENLY
JOY WOULDST COME MY WAY
I DARE'ST NOT DREAM LEST I A-WAKE AND
FIND THE SUN HAS VAN-ISHED MY
FE-ARS I CANS'T NOT BA-NISH AND
NOU-GHT BUT THE SUN WILL DIS- PEL
DARES'T NOT SLEEP LEST I SHOULD DREAM AND
FIND MY-SELF DI- MIN-ISHED MY
RE-VE-RIES UN- FIN-ISHED TO
BID MY PRE-TTY DREAM FARE-WELL I
C. Henle Verlag · HN 8046

TONI-LESLIE JAMES, COSTUME DESIGNER

"For the actors, every day, to come here and play dress-up," said producer Tonia Davis, "first with their incredible hair and makeup and then with the incredible costume department led by Toni-Leslie James, it allowed them to see themselves in the mirror as their characters hours before they had to go in front of the camera and be their characters every day. The costume is an integral part of how Colman transforms into Bayard, how Glynn transforms into Chief Randolph, and we're so lucky to be working with the heads of departments that we have. Toni-Leslie James has been just phenomenal. She and George have a shared language. As George put it to me once, she knew in her body exactly how 1963 was meant to look and feel on other people's bodies."

Audra McDonald spoke on the role of wardrobe, while on set in full costume: "You know wardrobe is everything, especially when you are doing a period work. And Toni-Leslie James—I've worked with her many times before—is a brilliant costume designer. And it informs you, even if you just think of it in terms of the fact that you feel like you can't move. If I'm truly going to move about in the space as Ella Baker, I can't be in jeans. I have to be in the clothing that she would have worn—and restricted—in the clothing that she would have worn, outfits for women of the '40s, '50s and '60s. Let's just say I'm not very comfortable right now because of things like the girdles and the slips and all of that, but it feels absolutely right for who Ella was."

Women's wardrobes in those years were designed to maintain certain kinds of images that women had to literally squeeze themselves into regardless of what paths they walked or what kind of work they did. The discomfort alone could become a preoccupation in those days. McDonald was struck by how little attention Baker paid to being stylish, but she still had no choice but to conform to how the clothes were made, which was uncomfortable. She wore what must have been a full head of hair in upswept hairdos, a salvation in the constant heat of the South. Her one flourish was to wear a pair of cat-eye sunglasses for outdoor rallies. Fannie Lou Hamer often wore outfits to give speeches that she may have worn to church, complete with a fancy hat, though they were not practical for the work she did in Mississippi. Gloria Richardson Dandridge, on the other hand, became famous in part by being photographed in the streets of her hometown in overalls adopted from the women of SNCC. Prior to the March, she was told by the NAACP that she needed to wear a dress, with a hat and gloves. She wore a jean skirt and sandals.[17]

Costume sketches by Toni-Leslie James.

But what is most striking about James's work is the necessity to dress an army of characters, almost all of whom were real persons, many of them famous, according to the many versions of self-expression shown by their clothing choices. "Toni's work has been amazing," said producer Mark Wright. "It was a tall order to dress so many people, to re-create the March on Washington, to re-create moments in time and find costumes that felt time appropriate but also provided character and color and texture to the world. She had to really dig deep and find these costumes, whether they were from New York or from California or from different shops in Pittsburgh or Ohio. She really left no stone unturned to have a library of a wardrobe and a deep closet to dress people. And Toni and her team did a fantastic job at all levels."

Wright observed the connection for actors between costume and building characters. "One thing that particularly stuck out to me was how George talked about wanting to portray Bayard through hair and costume, that Bayard didn't wear clothes—he threw them on. And you'll see throughout the film that he often has a relaxed look to his attire unless he's in a more formal setting, where clothes play a strong role in sending a message to the people in the room. And I think that attention to detail is really fascinating and a significant piece of the story."

One of the items Rustin evidently threw on was, to Colman Domingo, an inspired choice. "One of my favorite looks is actually his robe. I have a bathrobe, which is pretty extraordinary. They found this fabric in Pittsburgh and created this incredible robe that looks like a tapestry and feels royal. And I love that Toni-Leslie James, our costume designer, went with that fabric for when he's at home. When you're at home, it's less about the way the world sees you. Everyone goes out in a suit and tie, even if it's not your jam. But in his home, he's wearing this beautiful brocade robe that's long and gorgeous. And that's who he really is. So that's what I love, my favorite costume."

RUSTIN:
Thirty years ago Gandhi walked to the sea, picked up a handful of salt, and inspired a movement that brought down an empire. The time has come for us to do the same.

We are going to put together the largest peaceful gathering in the history of this nation, the world.

52 DELICIOUS VARIETIES
52 DELICIOUS VARIETIES

Costume sketches by Toni-Leslie James.

FREEDOM

MELISSA "MISSY" FORNEY, HEAD OF HAIR DEPARTMENT

Melissa Forney explained the hairstyle work as a collaboration. "I had worked with Colman before, and he didn't have any hair the first time I worked with him. When we started work on *Rustin*, he was filming in Austin, and I talked to him over the phone. He sent me photos, and I was like, 'Wow, he has hair.' But he didn't have enough hair for Rustin, so pieces were made for him. I got several different pieces, and when we did the test, that's when George selected what he wanted. Basically, that is the one that he wears in the film, the one that George chose. What we learned with George is that you really do have to pick his brain. He's great. His vision is out of this world. If he can't tell you what he wants, when he sees it, it's phenomenal. When you can get together with George and his vision, then it's like, man, we just created something. Together, as a team."

When Jeffrey Wright was asked what the film had to get right in portraying Adam Clayton Powell Jr., he responded: "Well, I think the hair above all else. The hair, the suit, and the mustache. I mean, he was very specific in his presentation. There's a kind of balance in who he was between outsized ego and a genuine, authentic commitment to the Civil Rights Movement and to the issues of the day. And so the key, I think, is trying to find the right balance between those seemingly opposite ends of the pole."

Actor Johnny Ramey described how his hairdo emerged: "I'm paying homage to Missy's father. The hair came because Missy's father was a preacher, and she loves her father. And so the part on the side, the low way the hair is laid down, the cut of the mustache and the soul patch, it's all to emulate someone who she loved desperately and who also was a preacher in life."

FOR
& FREEDOM

BEVERLY JO PRYOR, MAKEUP DEPARTMENT

"I started my research once I found out I was going to do the film," said Beverly Jo Pryor. "I read all the materials I could and studied everything in the time frame we were filming, even back to the 1940s, as well as the '60s and especially '63. It has been such a rewarding project and something I'm very proud to be a part of. I'm just trying to make it look as real and as authentic as I could. Whatever the time period is that you're working on, you have to carefully study that period. If a lot of makeup was worn, you put a lot of makeup on. This time period is more natural. A lot of makeup was not available back in the earlier days we are showing, so, of course, you're going to use it only to a certain extent. It's a collective effort. It takes everybody, no matter what your position, everybody on the set, every character, every team member, because you can't do it by yourself. It's always done collectively, especially makeup, hair, and wardrobe—they go hand in hand. We have to come together to make sure it all happens. Everybody has to help. Everybody's work is necessary."

Pryor was asked how she thinks the film may or may not fit into the current conversations about the ways in which history is taught in schools. "Well, this is part of history that has to be told, no matter what," she said. "It is going to have to fit in because it's reality, and it's even more real now. So, to me, it's going to fit in regardless. In this film, there is more than one type of struggle shown: a lack of equal rights for Blacks and disrespect for gays. It's reality. It's what people have got to understand. You can't judge. We're all part of God's creation."

LENNY KRAVITZ, SONGWRITER/PERFORMER OF THE ORIGINAL SONG "ROAD TO FREEDOM"

Multiple Grammy Award winner Lenny Kravitz contributed his talents to create the original song "Road to Freedom" for *Rustin*. He recounts, "I got a call from Bruce Cohen, who is one of the producers on the film. He and director George Wolfe thought that my music would be a good fit to the feeling of the film."

Asked about the source of his idea for the song, he said, "I drew my inspiration from the story of Bayard Rustin and the period in general. The Civil Rights Movement has always been important to me, as my mother educated me on it since I was a child. Then I let go, got out of the way, and let God inspire.

"Working with George," said Kravitz, "was intense and beautiful. He has a clear vision of what he wants. There was a lot of back and forth, lyrically and musically. For instance, he was very much inspired by the sound of the trombone choir and how that felt for him and the feeling of his images." Wolfe recalled this as well: "Ever since Branford Marsalis introduced me to a recording of the holy trombone choir from the United House of Prayer, I've been mesmerized. So when the brilliant, impassioned Lenny Kravitz agreed to write a song for *Rustin,* I begged him to include a chorus of trombones. Lenny took my request to the next level and brought on board the legendary Trombone Shorty. 'Road to Freedom' captures both 1963 and 2023—a bold celebration, as Lenny's voice sermonizes and soars."

Actor Colman Domingo also spoke about George's involvement: "Lenny is my brother. We met while shooting another monumental film, *Lee Daniels' The Butler*. When I found out that he was writing a song for our film, I called him immediately. He asked me for one thought to add to his brain trust for the song. All I could think of was the man that Rustin was and how it was most important to him that there was more work to be done. That was all that I could give. Lenny's warm voice said that he will let God speak through him to find the words, the melody, and ultimately the anthem. I love Lenny, and I am so thankful that he is a part of this gift of a film."

Kravitz described what he hopes audiences will take away from the film: "The story of Bayard Rustin. Most people do not know his story. It is beautiful and important. What he accomplished helped to change the situation in the most major way. Not only was he fighting for civil rights as a Black man, he was also fighting to be accepted as a Black gay man. His story deserves our attention and respect. 'Road to Freedom' says it for me. It is the path that my ancestors have been walking for so long. It is the path human beings have been walking since the beginning of time. We are all looking to be free mentally, physically, and spiritually."

KEEPERS OF THE FLAME

RACHELLE HOROWITZ

Rachelle Horowitz has a long track record as a strategist and organizer in the Civil Rights Movement and followed that with a long career in labor-union politics. While a college student in New York, she met Bayard Rustin volunteering with a group he was running. She worked on all the mobilizations that Rustin organized starting in the late 1950s. Rustin appointed the 24-year-old coordinator of all the transportation that the March groups would use—buses, trains, and planes—to bring people to the March on Washington. Following the March, she spent months in Mississippi helping to plan Freedom Summer and organizing the Freedom Democrats. She worked as Rustin's assistant from 1964 to 1973, and worked with him to form the Social Democrats, USA party. In the 1970s, she continued working with labor unions and was the political director of the American Federation of Teachers from 1974 to 1995.

Of her first meeting with Rustin, she recalled, "I went with Tom Kahn, who's portrayed in the movie. We were both in Brooklyn College and a friend of ours—we were both active politically—Michael Harrington, said, 'Go over to this office and work with Bayard Rustin.' So off we trotted. We were 17, and I mean, it's amazing historically, we walked into this small office on, I think, East or West 57th Street, and Bayard and Ella Baker were there, and they were raising money for the Montgomery Bus Boycott. Now, of course, one of the reasons we were there was that we were in college during the school integration in Little Rock. I mean, the Civil Rights Movement was burgeoning. And if you were in the North, you wanted to be part of it in some way and help. And there were people involved who were our age.

"So we became part of Bayard's coterie. And he nurtured us. Every time there was a protest or demonstration, off we'd trot to be part of it. And it was not unsystematic. Right during the Montgomery Bus Boycott, there was something called the Prayer Pilgrimage for Freedom [organized initially by Randolph]. It was in support of the boycott. But it was also a way for them to bring in other southern ministers so that it just wouldn't be Montgomery.

MARCH ON WASHINGTON
FOR
JOBS &
AUGUST 28, 1963

Bayard and A. Philip Randolph understood that it couldn't be one city alone. Then there were youth marches. They were little tiny models of what the March on Washington does. They were nonviolent. Dr. King always was the main speaker. There was a coalition of groups. That's how this movement grew. I mean, it was a training ground. So I would say from 1957 to 1963, at some point or other, I would go back to school. I would drop out of school. I'd go back to school. A whole bunch of us were primarily involved in the northern movement to support this burgeoning southern movement.

"The scene I really love in the film is when Bayard goes down to Atlanta to see Coretta King and to see Dr. King. And he gets into the house, and he winds up singing with Coretta and the kids. And that is the scene that I just loved because Colman, first of all, correctly and brilliantly, shows that other side of Bayard. This is not only the agitated leader. It also gives a little weight to Coretta and the role she played. I mean, there she is with these four kids, but I mean, she's doing whatever she can to make that house comfortable for Dr. King's protest. And that turned out to be my favorite scene in the movie."

Asked what she hoped audiences would get from the film, she said, "I hope they take away a feeling about Bayard, who is a part of history now and who was not then suitably honored. And I think that now they'll understand that he was courageous, persistent, that he overcame tremendous odds, and that he was a brilliant strategist."

From left: Tom Kahn, James Farmer, Ernest Green, and Rachelle Horowitz, members of the East River CORE, 1964.

WALTER NAEGLE

Bayard Rustin's partner, Walter Naegle, is the executive director of the Bayard Rustin Fund and a board member emeritus at the Bayard Rustin Center for Social Justice. Naegle accepted the Presidential Medal of Freedom on Rustin's behalf ten years ago from President Obama. He said, "Bayard's being awarded the Presidential Medal of Freedom during the 50th anniversary of the March on Washington for Jobs and Freedom was significant in a couple of ways. It brought him in from the 'margins' to join the Big Six leaders of the March, those men who headed the major civil rights organizations of that time. All of these men had received the medal before Bayard, despite the fact that he was the man who made the March the success that it was. The fact that only men were included in the Big Six was an error, given that women were the backbone of the movement. A representative of the National Council of Negro Women should have been part of the group. The fact that the award was presented by President Barack Obama, our first African American president, was also quite meaningful, and he acknowledged how Bayard had influenced his and the First Lady's own ideas.

"The occasion was also the first time that partners of LGBTQ+ Americans accepted the award on their deceased partner's behalf. Tam O'Shaughnessy, Sally Ride's partner, and I represented our spouses at the ceremony. The president's acknowledgment of our relationships was important to me personally, but also a recognition of the legitimacy of the loving bonds LGBTQ+ people have formed, despite all the forces against us. Love truly can conquer all. I was also happy to share the moment with family and friends who have worked to preserve and promote Bayard's legacy."

Bayard Rustin and his partner, Walter Naegle.

"To move the work forward 'angelically,' we must do it with a spirit of love, humility, forgiveness, and the hope of reconciliation, so that we can construct a better world."

WALTER NAEGLE

Asked what issues he thought Bayard Rustin would tackle today, Naegle said, "Broadly speaking, the elimination of poverty and the raising of the standard of living for all. Mr. Randolph, Bayard, and Dr. King all understood that many of the social ills we still face—drug addiction, petty crime, domestic violence, lack of quality education and health care—all stem from a lack of jobs that pay a living wage, and the absence of a strong commitment to the belief in 'people over profits.' In addition, and more specifically, he would be speaking out against attempts to diminish our democracy by restricting access to voting, passing laws to prevent people from living their authentic identities, and people turning their backs on the idea that truth exists—whether it be in how we report and analyze current events, or how we record them in history books. The process of 'seeking truth' is fundamental to Gandhian nonviolence, Bayard's Quakerism, and bringing about justice and reconciliation.

"What doesn't come through in most of the news footage of Bayard is that he was loving, generous, kind, and joyful. Yes, when he spoke in public, particularly at demonstrations, he could be fierce and militant, albeit nonviolently, but people who worked with him and knew him personally saw the other qualities I mentioned. Also, Bayard had a great appreciation for beauty, whether it was in words, music, or the visual arts."

Asked about his aspirations for *Rustin*, Naegle said, "I hope that audiences will take away a sense that Bayard was a person of dignity, integrity, principle, and courage—all qualities that he employed in the struggle to bring our country more in line with its founding ideals. I hope they will get a sense that movements are about masses of organized people, not individuals, and that while leaders arise, it is the foot soldiers that move the struggle forward. We all have a role we can play if we choose to do so."

On his reaction to the film, he said, "I think that George C. Wolfe did a masterful job of capturing the urgency of the moment, the tension in the society at the time of the March, while at the same time creating a human story of personal struggle, conflict, and, ultimately, redemption. Colman Domingo's portrayal of Bayard encompasses all of the qualities I mentioned—Bayard's militancy, his dignity, eloquence, and humanity. It is really a complete and complex portrayal that, I think, will inspire people to get involved in the struggle for civil and human rights."

Asked one thing that we can all do to carry on in Rustin's spirit, Naegle said: "First, and this is something Bayard always stressed, we must look within ourselves and recognize how we may be behaving cruelly or unjustly. We need to recognize, and accept, that we are all human beings capable of both good and evil. To move the work forward 'angelically,' we must do it with a spirit of love, humility, forgiveness, and the hope of reconciliation, so that we can construct a better world."

NATION
MARCH
FOR JOBS

HEADQUARTERS
N WASHINGTON
FREEDOM
WED. AUG.
28th

A LAST WORD

At age 74 in 1986, a year before his death, Bayard Rustin was asked how he would advise Black gay activists. The framing of the question prompted an answer from him that represents his work as an activist: "I think the most important thing I have to say is that they should try to build coalitions of people for the elimination of *all* injustice. Because if we want to do away with the injustice to gays, it will not be done because we get rid of injustice to gays. It will be done because we are forwarding the effort for the elimination of injustice to all. And we will win the rights for gays, or Blacks or Hispanics or women, within the context of whether we are fighting for all." In the years since the 1960s, we have seen a profusion of groups dedicated to causes from school violence, police violence, and partisan gerrymandering targeting specific communities, to drives to purge schools and libraries of books that address our various experiences. With the death of George Floyd, we saw people who support one or more of these fights together in the streets, because injustice to one is dangerous to all.

One of the many beauties of the film *Rustin* is that we see this coalition in formation as Bayard Rustin builds his team in 1963, as he recruits young people, as one or two elders protect him from being personally targeted by politics, and, finally, as the multitude of human beings of every description throng the National Mall to demand justice for the nation's citizens. Within the film's breadth we see the beauty and complexity of a man who never checked his watch to see what time it was because it was always the right time, and he was in a marathon relay and his eyes were on passing the baton.

Following pages: (right) Crowd assembled on the Mall during the civil rights March on Washington for Jobs and Freedom, 1963.

WE
MARCH
FOR

We Work For
FREEDOM,
BUT
TO BE FREE
WE NEED
TO WORK
WE
MARCH
FOR
FIRST CLASS
CITIZENSHIP
NOW!
WE
MARCH
FOR
FIRST CLASS
CITIZENSHIP
NOW!
WE
MARCH
FOR
EFFECTIVE
CIVIL RIGHTS
LAWS
NOW!
WE
DEMAND
DECENT
HOUSING

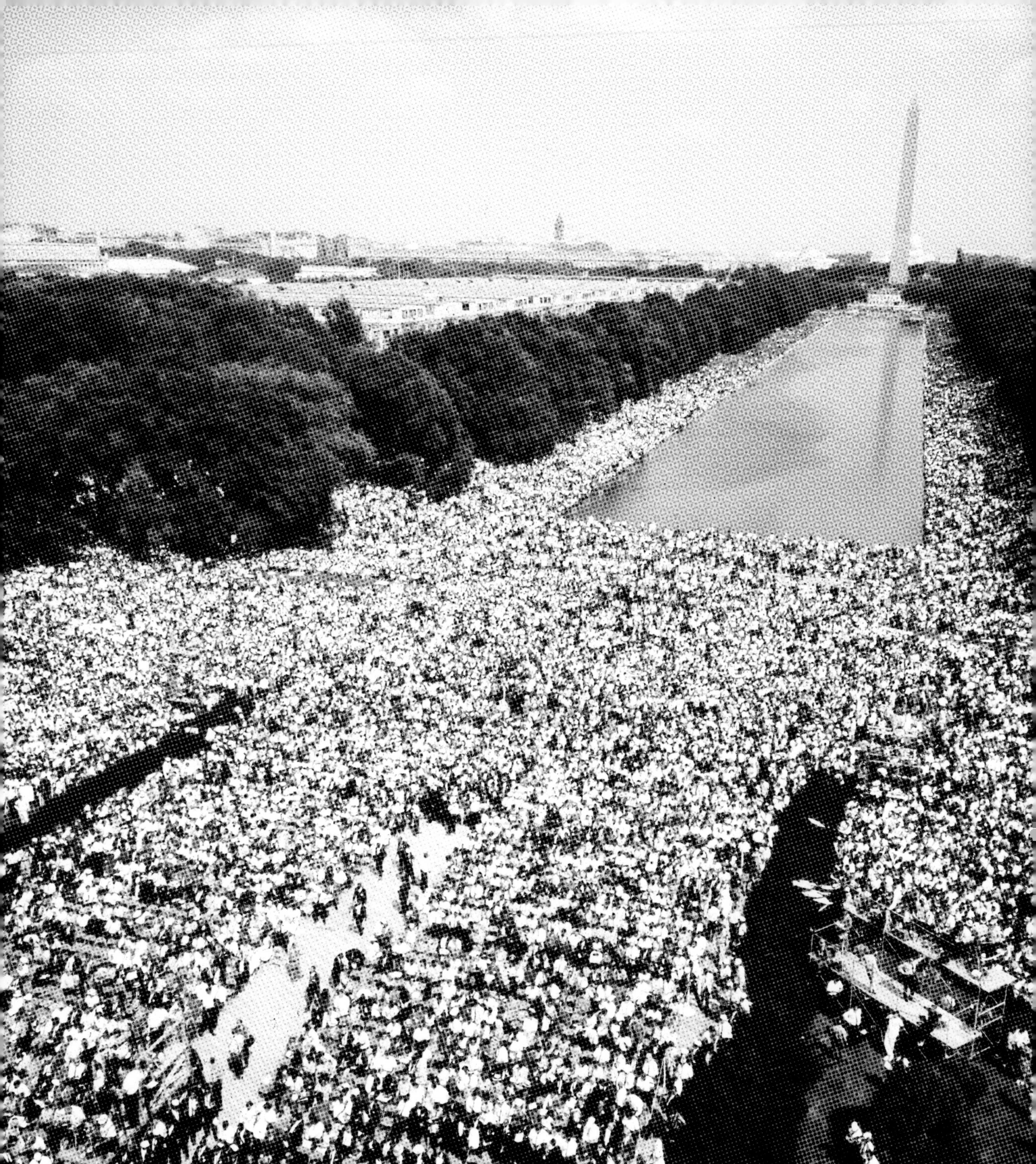

“When an individual is protesting society’s refusal to acknowledge his dignity as a human being, his very act of protest confers dignity on him.”

BAYARD RUSTIN

Marchers cheer after Martin Luther King Jr.’s “I Have a Dream” speech at the March on Washington, 1963.

ABOUT THE AUTHOR

Thulani Davis is an interdisciplinary artist and scholar who is an associate professor and a Nellie Y. McKay Fellow in the African American Studies Department at the University of Wisconsin-Madison. She has had a long career in journalism while creating work in poetry and theater that includes plays and libretti for four operas. She has written the scripts for several award-winning documentaries, including Louis Massiah's *W. E. B. Du Bois: A Biography in Four Voices* (1996) and Massiah's short film *In Ragtime: James Reese Europe* (2011), and she developed the concept for Blackside's series *I'll Make Me a World: A Century of African American Arts* (1999). She also wrote the script for the narrative film *Paid in Full* (2002). She is the author of six books, the most recent of which is *The Emancipation Circuit: Black Activism Forging a Culture of Freedom* (2022).

ACKNOWLEDGMENTS

George C. Wolfe, Bruce Cohen, Tonia Davis, Mark R. Wright, Barack Obama, Michelle Obama, Julian Breece, Dustin Lance Black, Colman Domingo, Chris Rock, Glynn Turman, Aml Ameen, CCH Pounder, Michael Potts, Jeffrey Wright, Audra McDonald, Tobias Schliessler, Mark Ricker, Branford Marsalis, Lenny Kravitz, Toni-Leslie James, Melissa Forney, Beverly Jo Pryor, Rachelle Horowitz, Walter Naegle, Thulani Davis, Faith Childs, Inside Projects, William A. Wolfe, Mellesia Miller, Lisa Taback, Michelle Douvris, Chris Gonzalez, Sara Reich, Stacey Browning, Sue Warde, Sarah Rodman, Jennifer Eckstein, Nicole LaCoursiere, Norell Giancana, Kyle Bonnici, and the great Bayard Rustin.

The publisher would like to thank the folllowing: Stephen Watt, Adelman Images; Jessica Halliday, akg-images; Don Davis, American Friends Service Committee; Maria Fernanda Pessaro, Artists Rights Society; Matthew Lutts, Associated Press; Courtland Cox; Estate of Bayard Rustin; Susan H. Smith, Ethan Vesely-Flad, Fellowship of Reconciliation; Florida Memory, State Archives of Florida; Clifton Franklin; Brian Stehlin, Getty Images; Jermaine Jackson Jr.; Kimberly Katz, Shutterstock.

FOOTNOTES

1. John D'Emilio, *Lost Prophet: The Life and Times of Bayard Rustin,* 12.
2. D'Emilio, 26.
3. Devon W. Carbado & Donald Weise, eds. *Time on Two Crosses: The Collected Writings of Bayard Rustin,* Cleis Press Inc., 2003, xii.
4. Carbado & Weise, xii-xiii; D'Emilio, 32-34.
5. D'Emilio, 32: "Barney Josephson, Owner of Café Society Jazz Club Is Dead at 86," *The New York Times,* Sept. 30, 1988, Section B, p. 9 [accessed 6/28/23]. https://www.nytimes.com/1988/09/30/obituaries/barney-josephson-owner-of-cafe-society-jazz-club-is-dead-at-86.html?pagewanted=all
6. D'Emilio, 406.
7. D'Emilio, 327.
8. Bond was a co-founder of SNCC and of the Southern Poverty Law Center, and in the '60s and '70s was elected to the Georgia State House and State Senate. He was one of the first African Americans elected to state office since the end of black voting in the state in the 1900s.
9. D'Emilio, 329-30.
10. D'Emilio, 338.
11. D'Emilio, 351.
12. John Lewis, "Together, You Can Redeem the Soul of Our Nation," *The New York Times,* July 30, 2020.
13. D'Emilio, 195, 297.
14. Barbara Ransby, *Ella Baker & the Black Freedom Movement: A Radical Democratic Vision,* University of North Carolina, 2003, pp.179-83.
15. Barbara Ransby, *Ella Baker & the Black Freedom Movement: A Radical Democratic Vision,* University of North Carolina, 2003, 4, 142, 154, 162, 176, 314.
16. Joseph R. Fitzgerald, *The Struggle Is Eternal: Gloria Richardson and Black Liberation,* University Press of Kentucky, 2018, 127.
17. Fitzgerald, 125.

TEXT CREDITS

Devon W. Carbado & Donald Wise, eds. *Time on Two Crosses: The Collected Writings of Bayard Rustin,* foreword by Barack Obama, afterword by Barney Frank, Cleis Press, 2015.

John D'Emilio, *Lost Prophet: The Life and Times of Bayard Rustin,* Free Press, 2003.

Joseph R. Fitzgerald, *The Struggle Is Eternal: Gloria Richardson and Black Liberation,* University of Kentucky, 2018.

Henry Hampton and Steve Fayer, *Voices of Freedom: An Oral History of the Civil Rights Movement from the 1950s through the 1980s,* Bantam, 1990.

Michael G. Long, ed., *I Must Resist: Bayard Rustin's Life in Letters,* foreword by Julian Bond, City Lights Books, 2012.

Ransby, Barbara, *Ella Baker & The Black Freedom Movement: A Radical Democratic Vision,* University of North Carolina, 2003.

CREDITS

Film stills by Tobias Schliessler.
Unit photography by David Lee, Parrish Lewis and Jon Pack.

Page 6: © Kevin Dietsch/picture-alliance/dpa/AP Images; p. 9: © Fellowship Records (FOR), digital photo courtesy of Walter Naegle/Estate of Bayard Rustin; p. 13: Photography by Orlando Fernandez for *The New York World-Telegram & Sun*, Prints and Photographs Division, Library of Congress, LC-DIG-ppmsca-35538; p. 18: © Eddie Adams/AP Photo; p. 21: © A. Camerano/AP Photo; p. 23: © Ed Clarity/*New York Daily News* Archive/Getty Images; p. 26: © Bettmann/Getty Images; p. 27: © 2011 - 2023 Student Nonviolent Coordinating Committee (SNCC) Legacy Project/All Rights Reserved; pp. 55, 232: © Flip Schulke/Corbis/Getty Images; p. 64: Mark R. Wright, Bruce Cohen, Tonia Davis and Alex G. Scott; p. 79: Julian Breece and Dustin Lance Black; p. 86 (bottom): Photography by Harry H. Haworth/Courtesy of American Friends Service Committee; p. 104: © Francis Miller/The LIFE Picture Collection/Shutterstock; pp. 108, 229: © Robert W. Kelley/The LIFE Picture Collection/Shutterstock; p. 115: © MPI/Getty Images; p. 116: © Leonard Mccombe/The LIFE Picture Collection/Shutterstock; p. 125: © 2023 Estate of Fred Stein/Artists Rights Society (ARS), New York, digital photo © Fred Stein/picture-alliance/akg-images; p. 131: © Arthur Brower/*New York Times* Co./Getty Images; p. 140: © AP Photo; p. 143: © Grey Villet/The LIFE Picture Collection/Shutterstock; p. 151: © Afro American Newspapers/Gado/Getty Images; p. 154: © Harry Harris/AP Photo; p. 159: © Dick Strobel/AP Photo; p. 160: (top) © Thomas D. Mcavoy/The LIFE Picture Collection/Shutterstock, (bottom) © Afro American Newspapers/Gado/Getty Images; p. 161: (top) © Tony Pescatore/*New York Daily News* Archive/Getty Images, (bottom) © William J. Smith/AP Photo; p. 162: (top) © Francis Miller/The LIFE Picture Collection/Shutterstock, (bottom) Courtesy of Clifton Franklin; p. 163: (top) © Bettmann/Getty Images, (bottom) © Universal History Archive/UIG/Getty Images; pp. 177, 182 (top, middle), 183: Mark Ricker; p. 191: (bottom left) Branford Marsalis, (bottom right) Rod Ward; pp. 193 (bottom row), 200: Toni-Leslie James; p. 210: Courtesy of Lenny Kravitz; p. 216: © Bob Adelman; pp. 218-219: Courtesy of Walter Naegle/Estate of Bayard Rustin; p. 236: © Jermaine Jackson Jr.

Every possible effort has been made to identify and contact all rights holders and obtain their permission for work appearing in these pages. Any errors or omissions brought to the publisher's attention will be corrected in future editions.

All interviews with participants were captured before May 2023.

Front cover: Unit photography by David Lee.
Back cover: Bayard Rustin during a news conference at the March on Washington New York City headquarters, 1963. © AP Photo.
Front endpages: (*left*) Film still by Tobias Schliessler. (*card insert, right*) Reproduction of a mail-in participation pledge for the March on Washington for Jobs and Freedom on August 28, 1963. Courtesy of Florida Memory, State Archives of Florida, Collection N2015-1.

Senior editor: Scout Sabo
Designer: Dylan Brackett
Senior photo editor: Andrea Ramírez Reyes
Photo editor: Claire Ruch
Production manager: Nico Sidoti

3 Park Avenue, 27th floor
New York, NY 10016 USA
Tel: 212-989-6769   Fax: 212-647-0005
assouline.com

Printed in Italy by Grafiche Milani.
ISBN: 9781649803160